# FORENSIC
# PSYCHOLOGY

# FORENSIC PSYCHOLOGY

A Guide for Lawyers and
the Mental Health
Professions

## Robert Gordon,
J.D., Ph.D.

NELSON-HALL/Chicago

*In memory of M. G. Gordon,*
*father, teacher, and friend*

*Forensic Psychology* was originally published by
Lawyers and Judges Publishing Company in 1975.

**Library of Congress Cataloging in Publication Data**
Gordon, Robert, 1944
    Forensic psychology.
    Reprint of the 1975 ed. published by Lawyers and
Judges Pub. Co., Tucson.
    Includes index.
    1.  Psychology, Forensic.  2.  Evidence, Expert—
United States.  I.  Title.
KF8965.G6 1975    347'.73'66        77-1452
ISBN 0–88229–477–6

# contents

# introduction

The creative and effective lawyer of the future will have a working understanding of the field of psychology, will develop a working relationship with the mental health team in his community and state, so that he may utilize their skills for the benefit of his clients. The purpose of this book is three fold: first, to provide the practicing lawyer with a new perspective concerning his services, clients, and role in society; second, to provide him with specific examples in both criminal and civil cases where psychologists aid in the resolution of psychological and societal issues; and third, to give psychologists, psychiatrists and social workers illustrations of the types of cases in which their consultation will be valuable to members of the legal profession so as to help them prepare for what the attorney and court will expect of them.

To fulfill these purposes, a practical, problem-solving approach is employed. The earlier an attorney begins to work with the forensic approach to law, the more comfortable he becomes with its technique. This idea struck home to me from a course which Professor Walter Steele and I offered at Southern Methodist University School of Law, entitled, "Legal Counseling and Interviewing Techniques." The reactions of former students now practicing have been enthusiastic. The course involved scenarios of attorney-client interviews which students were asked to role-play. The interviews were video-taped for later discussion. We coached the "client," but left the student lawyer in the dark. Each case presented a superficial legal problem, but the best resulting advice was psycho-legal in nature. Scenario examples are: the patent applicant who is actually paranoid schizophrenic; the father who seeks child custody out of guilt, but who actually doesn't want to win; and the client who can't sign her will because of anxiety over dying.

A compelling motive for every attorney is to build a larger practice by helping clients whose problems fall in areas which are of interest to him. This result is not solely achieved by "winning" cases. If we isolate winning cases from the general quality and effectiveness of practice, winning becomes a matter of chance or luck. More often than not, winning actually means negotiating a plea or settlement which makes the client happy. Often my patients who must serve jail time or who receive meager damage awards maintain the highest regard for their lawyers and will call on them in the future because they feel that the attorney cared about them personally, and did everything under the law to help them.

The setting for this book is the legal process and in this theater, the attorney is front and center. The book has a theme—law is man—a working theory which prescribes that in order to understand law, it is first necessary to understand the men and women who create, interpret and practice it. Thus, to understand the Civil Rights Act of 1964, we must understand the men and women of congress at that time. To understand the subpoena of Richard Nixon's tapes, we must understand Judge John Sirica, and to understand the defense in the Scopes Monkey Trial, we must understand Clarence Darrow.

For the attorney to understand law from the forensic perspective, he must grope to understand himself, his drives, emotional states and lifestyle as he directly experiences them and as society expects him to. This does not mean the attorney should undergo intensive psychotherapy, but he should subject himself to critical self-analysis. Legal assumptions which are unconsciously internalized are challenged in this book. Concepts such as "burden of proof" and "the reasonable man" do not always mirror the reality. A fact for one man, is a question for another, or may not even exist for a third. One cannot be insightful toward clients, witnesses or courts, if one lacks knowledge of himself.

In the chapter, "View From The Bench," the Court is viewed as a man subject to the same psychological experiences as other men. The charisma and mystery are stripped away. When the judge's needs and motives are appreciated, it is possible to relate to him in a nonthreatened and nonthreatening way, which as a psychological issue sometimes jeopardizes an otherwise favorable verdict. Members of the judiciary are also becoming sensitive to the psychological effects of their holdings. In 1974, Oswin Chrisman, a progressive and insightful domestic relations judge in Dallas, Texas, participated in a study which I designed in order to determine whether litigants in his court believed they were treated fairly, and whether they subjectively believed that justice was done. Out of 200 litigants studied, 71% of the males, and 94% of the females believed the outcome was fair and just. We were unable to analyze these findings with reference to "plaintiffs" and "defendants" since over 80% of the divorce case litigants in our study believed themselves to be defendants.

In "Jury Selection," the myths of voir dire are exploded, such as "narrow eyes suggest secretiveness" or "a thin upper lip responds to charm." In its place is substituted an empirical, scientific approach which emphasizes the prediction of juror behavior, and which rejects mere speculation after the verdict is in. In this chapter, I will discuss the approach I developed in cases which yielded the largest damage awards to date for personal injury cases in Dallas and Houston, Texas, and the approach used in the celebrated Cundiff murder trial.

In "How Evidence Is Perceived," the social-psychological aspects of perception are discussed and explained, special attention is paid to those techniques which allow oral testimony and demonstrative evidence to be more realistic, poignant, understandable and persuasive. All too often, trial attorneys ignore the fact that photographs of murder victims, like pictorial representations of accident scenes are perceived differently by different jurors. During the Watergate hearings, the almost photographic memory of accuser John Dean, contrasted sharply with testimony given by White House Assistant, Dick Moore, who had difficulty recalling certain incidents which occurred the same day as his testimony. But for all its blanks and inconsistencies, Mr. Moore's statement was more realistic.

Modern psychology and law have now passed the stage of mutual antagonism and mistrust. They are complementary. Forensic psychology as perspective has grown in usefulness considerably since the time Dean Wigmore relegated it to a footnote in his multi-volume work on evidence. Theoretical and empirical differences between psychology and the law will and should remain so long as psychology seeks the truth through empirical science and the law seeks it through a humanistic adversary process. Beyond the law is man concept, a second theme for this book is called "the psycho-legal syndrome," which states that there is no such thing as a legal or psychological problem, only a human problem with a more dominant judicial or social characteristic. Reading an applied psychology book will not transform an attorney into a psychologist. An attorney by choice and training, is prepared to practice law, not psychology. But the effective attorney of the future will learn how to use psychological knowledge and insight in helping his clients, and in developing a more effective practice.

# acknowledgements

I am grateful to the following individuals who reviewed this manuscript, offered helpful comments, or who have had a significant impact on my understanding of the conceptual relationship between psychology and law and its practical clinical applications:

Dr. Verner Baugh
Judge Oswin Chrisman
Mrs. Lynn Dewitt
Judge Fran Goodwin
Mr. Victor L. Gumma
Judge Clarence Guittard
Judge Robert Hamilton
Dr. Bob Hood
James Marshall, Attorney at Law
Dr. Michael Nash

Dr. Jay Powell
Mr. Ted Repshoult
Professor Gian Sarup
Professor Walter Steele
Robert C. Sullivan, Attorney at Law
Professor Ted Talbot
Dr. Maurice K. Temerlin
Michael J. Vaughn, Attorney at Law
Professor Clemente Vivanco

The beautiful and subtle drawings which illustrate the introductory page of each chapter were drawn by the artist Montarier. A catalogue of his works is available by writing Nora Gallery, 9 Maimon Ave., Jerusalem, Israel. The creative illustrations of gestural behavior of judges were drawn by Dallas, Texas artist Ron Anderson.

I thank my wife, Sue, for her insightful suggestions at every phase of manuscript preparation, for her emotional support and patience.

I thank my daughter, Amy, for being Amy.

# FORENSIC
# PSYCHOLOGY

# chapter 1

# A Lawyer's Reflection

Montázier 75

| | |
|---|---|
| Psychologist: | Think seriously about the question I'm going to ask you. Try to answer it as honestly as possible. . . |
| | Who are you? |
| Attorney: | Well, as you know, I'm William H. Scott. |
| Psychologist: | Bill, I didn't ask your name. I asked who "you" were. |
| Attorney: | I'm a lawyer. |
| Psychologist: | That's your profession, isn't it? |
| Attorney: | *(Pause)* I'm a Christian. |
| Psychologist: | Now that's your religion. |
| Attorney: | I'm a thirty-four year old man. |
| Psychologist: | In that statement, you've described your position along the evolutionary scale, your sex and age, but not who you really are. |
| Attorney: | I'm an American citizen. . . I guess I'm really . . . |
| Psychologist: | What I'm asking is - what is uniquely you. . . different perhaps from me and everyone else. |
| Attorney: | Sometimes I think you psychologists have problems facing reality. But I must admit, it's a fascinating question. Now, how would you like to take the witness stand? |

The purpose of this book is to view the legal process and its protagonist, the attorney, through the aperture of forensic psychology, a discipline which relates psychology and law. The resulting perspective will contribute and increase the effectiveness of the legal practitioner. Since we place the attorney as an individual at the center of our concern, instead of the rule of law, this idea becomes dynamic. Traditional approaches to understanding law have always emphasized law as codified rules of norms which regulate the behavior of men in society; in other words, "the law is the law is the law." As a freshman law student I became acquainted with this approach during the first course in criminal law taught by a criminal district judge. After he announced the rule that gory pictures could not be shown to a jury because it would inflame them, I raised my hand. "If the picture reflects the reality," I asked, "why not show it to the jury?" "That's a stupid question," snapped the judge, "the law's the law and that's good enough for me."

Law has also been characterized as "process" developing out of the sociological jurisprudence of Dean Pound and more recent exposition by Yale Professors McDougal and Lasswell. Forensic psychology rejects the "law as process" concept as it does the "law is the law" concept. It favors instead, the "law as man theory." This theory brings to jurisprudence, the empirical referents, the "nitty gritty" of legal experience. Its premise is that to best understand law, one must understand the men and women who create, practice and interpret it. It defines law as what the Supreme Court says it is; it defines legal practice as that which attorneys do or say they do; and it suggests that a case style such as Williamson vs. Kentworth should more accurately reflect the names of the attorneys who prepared, argued and appealed the rights and obligations of the litigants themselves.

From this new and emergent perspective, the attorney who wishes to increase his understanding of law and his professional effectiveness, must first increase his understanding of himself and his colleagues, judges and legislators in terms of the following mental and emotional functions: frame of reference, motivational structure, emotional effect and self concept.

The psychologist-attorney dialogue began with the question, "Who are you?" Although many attorneys have considerable psychological insight, until recently, very few have formally studied forensic psychology.[1] Attorney Bill Scott would have preferred a question about the validity of holographic wills, new approaches to products liabilities, or the constitutional infringements of administrative agencies. A satisfactory answer to the "who are you" question involves developmental analysis of one's life style, which begins at conception, not with admission to law school. Such analysis especially focuses on adolescent experience which is embroiled with decision making about life's three most meaningful choices: What will I be (occupation)? Who will I marry (or more recently, who will I live with)? What kind of human being do I want to become? Whom one marries and occupational choice are often interrelated. Spouses can help catapult an attorney into successful practice especially in those cases where an attorney is technically competent but lacks the personality to attract clients. But from clinical experience, I know that a wife who is jealous or resentful of her husband's career can sabotage it in a variety of ways. Among the attorneys I have seen in therapy, no one adolescent motivation factor emerges as the reason for choosing a career in law. One bright municipal lawyer who came from a poor family was driven by a desire "to make something of myself." Another who is a prosecutor, lacked a stable father figure and identified with his father-in-law, a successful trial lawyer. Still another became a lawyer because he decided he couldn't earn a living playing chess.

Attorney Bill Scott responded typically to the "who am I" dialogue by defining himself with reference to surname, profession, specie, nationality, sex and age. His reference points were attempts to locate himself in time and space, in socio-economic class and in history. Also quite normally, he attacked the source of discomfort, the psychologist, no doubt relying on historical legal precedent. At

---

1. Colleges and universities currently offering courses in psychology and law or law and society are: Flordia State University, Harvard, George Washington University, UCLA, University of Southern California, State of Michigan Center for Forensic Psychiatry, University of Nebraska, University of Rochester Medical School, University of Michigan, Temple University, University of Alabama, Menninger Foundation, University of Pittsburgh, Case Western Reserve University, Southern Methodist University, University of Colorado, University of Maryland.

the turn of the century, Advocate Charles Moore announced that he would rather have Sherlock Holmes himself in court than a psychologist; and even more contemporary practitioners have at times dismissed psychological knowledge and insight with the blow of a single phrase, "human nature being what it is." Nevertheless, Bill Scott's ego strength was sufficient that he recognized the question's fascination.

The time and space coordinates Mr. Scott used to describe or define himself are significant because they provide indications of the nature of his personal frame of reference and its stability. A frame of reference is a complex psychological phenomenon composed of personality variables such as attitudes, past experience, self concept, motivational levels, emotional characteristics and intelligence. The frame of reference is not a physical structure, but a psychological function. For example, by surgically removing a section of cranium and by visually exploring the gray matter of the cortex, one can never find the hypothesized personality structures of Sigmund Freud, namely, the Id, Ego or Superego. That is not to say that physical localization of personality processes will not be possible in the future. Psychiatrists and neuro-psychologists can already locate areas of the brain associated with thought, vision, hearing, psychomotor coordination, and basic areas of emotion.

Consider the following example of how the frame of reference actually affects our behavior. It is evening on a quiet suburban street. The street is part of a new housing development, and street lights have not yet been installed. Walking to get some exercise, an attorney notices a new Mercedes parked near the curb. As he approaches, he notices the right front window rolled down one third of the way. He begins to fantasize, "If the car were stolen, the thief might drive to another city or leave the state, remove the license plates, scratch out the engine serial number and then try to sell it to an unscrupulous dealer. When the owner returned and realized the car was stolen, he would probably call the police and then his insurance agent or maybe vice versa. Assuming the car wasn't recovered, the owner would seek compensation from the insurance company for the full market value of the car, plus loss of convenience and use. The insurance adjuster, in an effort to protect his loss ratio would ask him whether at the time of the theft, the car doors were locked and the windows rolled up. Then the agent would begin to accumulate evidence of negligence on the owner's part, perhaps barring recovery under the contract for coverage. Hmm. . . . Those standard form contracts. ."

The attorney's fantasy elicited by the hypothetical situation is logical, rational, and predictable in terms of his frame of reference. Particularly operative is the role of attitudes held and past experiences. Assume a psychologist whose training and experience provides a sharp contrast to the attorney's, is walking down the same street under the same conditions and on the same evening. Can't we predict a vastly different fantasy? The psychologist would be more likely to think, "Here is a fancy car belonging to a typical, middle class suburbanite groping for status. He is upwardly mobile, lives beyond the outer perimeter of the city, commutes to work, lives beyond his means and frets about inflation. He is probably a warm and accepting person, extroverted and not overly concerned about the possibility of someone's stealing his car. On the other hand, from the viewpoint of Freudian personality theory, it is possible that he is actually inviting someone to steal his car, a kind of seduction for friendship, belonging or sex. Hmmm. . . Why did I assume the owner to be male?"

## Bio-Social Factors

The frame of reference is capable of quantification or measurement and it is focal and critical to understanding human behavior and experience. Within the frame of reference are "points" or "anchors" representing groups in society which the individual identifies with and aspires to relate to. These are his reference groups. Also, within the frame of reference field are membership groups which the individual belongs to, but doesn't necessarily identify with. Consequently, the latter do not influence behavior or shape attitudes in a very significant way. An attorney may be a member in good standing, and regularly attend meetings of the local Chamber of Commerce, Elks Club and Kiwanis, primarily because he believes that he should become involved in civic affairs and because it affords him an opportunity for visability to meet prospective clients; but he is only peripherally committed to their goals and values and only indirectly affected by their attitudes. Such groups are his membership groups. His church group, local bar or country club, may affect his attitudes and behavior in a more direct way, thereby constituting a reference group.

Another anchoring point is composed of societal expectations about how the lawyer should look and talk and act; and the bio-social approach to personality emphasizes that these expectations structure how the individual perceives himself. The typical, middle class community member views the attorney as a writer of wills, someone to see when the cleaners ruin a fur coat or when the chain store credit department annoys him about what he believes are unfair charges. He is someone to see when son Ralph steals a car or daughter Sandy is caught at high school with marijuana traces in her coat. He is a writer of contracts when purchasing a home and a reviewer of abstracts where the title company doesn't talk the buyer into title insurance instead. This middle class stereotype is different from the classical working class perception of the attorney as one who is too busy and too expensive to handle his problems. The working class individual views the attorney as the forecloser, the landlord, the repossessor — an agent of the upper class. Despite the establishment of legal aid clinics and experimental programs of prepaid legal services (Judicare), the working class perception is not inaccurate. The attorney is generally the spokesman and counsel for the upper and middle classes who can afford to hire him.

By the time they reach college, most Americans will have spent as much time in front of the T.V. as in school. The middle class stereotype of the attorney, captured and projected by T.V. programming, becomes familiar. During the 1960's it was "Judd for the Defense," "The Defenders," "Perry Mason," "The Bold Ones" and "The Law and Mr. Jones." During the early 1970's it was "Owen Marshall" and "Petrocelli." Such Hollywood characterizations feed back to the middle class an unrealistic, however flattering depiction of the attorney. On these shows, no one ever asks for a fee and the distinct impression is given that the attorney serves his client asking only altruistic self satisfaction in return.

Television depicts the attorney as an aggressive, sensitive and articulate specialist in criminal law, psychology and detective work. If T.V. attorneys are not young, they are virile and enjoy the deepest possible personal relationship with their secretaries short of on screen sexual involvement. The programs thus far produced are obsessed with romance in the courtroom, the revelation of truth, the ultimate moment of guilt or innocence, the release of aggression and the plight of the underdog, miraculously saved by the brilliant communicative skills of the lawyer and the bumbling, futile protestations of the opposing counsel. Never a glimpse of months of fact gathering, legal research, and seemingly endless days of mundane testimony, evidence and appeal preparation is shown. All is compressed into 60 minutes of prime time minus breath-purifying, stomach-settling, and whiter-than-white laundry commercials. Most incredulous is the continuous background of music reaching crescendo at moments of climax, involving innocent, beautiful defendants, white haired sagacious judges and handsome, confident defense counsel. Still, it seems unlikely that the T.V. audience would tolerate more realistic though mundane programs whose subject matter are suits in breach of contract under the Uniform Commercial Code, suits to remove clouds from titles to real property, or suits to recover on promissory notes.

The danger of course, lurks when the attorney believes he must distort his behavior to match the T.V. stereotype. Clients and jurors react with hostility to affections. In a "Psychology and the Law" class which I teach to non-lawyers, I asked two attorneys to present plaintiff and defense arguments in a medical malpractice case in which a patient was placed in restraints since psychiatric hospital attendents believed she was having an anxiety attack. Actually, she was having an asthma attack and died within 24 hours. Attorney A, who fancied himself a trial lawyer, stated the plaintiff's case with a dynamic, folksy, anecdote laden T.V. style. Attorney B, who had a largely office practice, emphasized the issues and tried conscientiously not to draw attention to himself. On a seven point scale, the class gave both attorneys a 6 plus rating on competency, but gave lawyer B a higher rating on the factors of "sincerity" and "overall effectiveness."

The tendency to perceive oneself in terms of stereotypic community expectations was dramatically illustrated by Dr. M. K. Temerlin, a psychologist at the University of Oklahoma. Temerlin announced to his psychology of personality class that his assistants were studying personality evaluations and would analyze and prepare a report on each student's personality. Each student was asked to draw a picture of a man which, they were told, would form the basis of the diagnosis. Three weeks passed. Each student was given a sealed envelope, personally addressed. Enclosed was their personality evaluation. The students were then asked to rate the accuracy and validity of the evaluations. In other words, how well they thought the evaluations described them. The results are shown on this page. The skewed distribution indicates that a significant number of the students believed that the evaluations were extremely accurate.

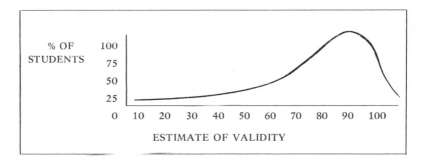

Immediately after class, one young man rushed to the podium and blurted to the professor that being in therapy for two years never produced such insightful diagnosis. Temerlin asked for a student volunteer to read his evaluation aloud for "the benefit of science." As a pretty coed volunteer cleared her throat, then read with gravity, the lecture hall began to buzz with amazement, student exchanging glances with student, as they realized that each of them was given the exact same personality description.

If the attorney internalizes the T.V. stereotpye, he runs the risk of being labeled "insincere" as well as self-deceiving, but when he internalizes the negative lawyer stereotpye, he may destroy his career. The prevailing nega-stereotype of the attorney views him as incompetent, scheming and dishonest. In *The Trouble With Lawyers,* Murry T. Bloom, journalist and author, devotes an entire chapter to the observation, "Why we don't like lawyers." His book reports characterizations of the attorney as a technician who is "stupid, lazy or inept" as a thief who mishandles his clients' money, demands unreasonable fees and who views divorce as good business. In support of these allegations, Bloom cites a Missouri Bar study.[2]

- Most people rated lawyers below bankers, clergy, doctors, dentists and teachers in "general reputation." People who used a lawyer thought less highly of them than did people who never used one.
- Only 35 percent of the people thought lawyers were honest and truly dedicated to their profession.
- About 40 percent of the public believed lawyers' bills were too high.
- Most people—nearly 70 percent—believed that the basis for a lawyer's fee should be the "effort expended." (Obviously, this means that the public is against bar minimum fee schedules that provide a percentage fee for legal work in probate, personal injury, real estate, divorce or sale of a business. But the survey analysts delicately didn't go into the public opposition to percentage fees.)
- Most of the public and the lawyers themselves believed contingent fees in personal injury cases were much too high. Many of the complaints about lawyers overcharging came from people in the Kansas City area where the prevailing contingent fee in personal injury cases is 50 percent. Most people thought 25 percent or less would be fair.
- Nearly 57 percent of the people who used lawyers thought lawyers created lawsuits unnecessarily, that they didn't make enough effort to settle cases out of court as they should.

2. Murry T. Bloom, THE TROUBLE WITH LAWYERS, New York, Simon and Schuster, 1968.

- Most shocking to the survey's conductors was the finding that almost 12 percent of the people who used lawyers were solicited for their cases, mainly in personal injury matters. Since soliciting is an ethical violation that could—but seldom does—lead to disbarment, a lot of Missouri lawyers are practicing who shouldn't be.

The fact that Bloom's book was marketed successfully indicates the potency of the negative stereotype. Even some lawyers reacted favorably. Although individuals resent personal criticism, there is a propensity on the part of some to enjoy being criticized as a group. One cynic suggested that if the inhabitants of earth decided to begin a new society on the moon, a feasibility study of the function and responsibilities of members of the new society would not provide a single attorney with a space ship ticket. Maybe so. But arguments among members of the new society and antisocial conduct would erupt. Rules or norms for behavior would be proposed, then consensual agreement would follow. Ultimately, these norms would become written down or codified. Those members who knew more about the nature and application of these codified norms would probably be called "wise men," or even "lawyers."

Medicare and Medicaid abuses have tarnished the professional image of medical doctors; misapplication of psychological testing in government and industry has led to E.E.O.C. regulations and the Griggs vs. Duke Power Co. landmark decision. Similarly, unethical practices by some attorneys impugn the integrity of the legal profession. In so far as the law student and the young attorney in practice begin to identify with the caveat emptor doctrine of legal practice and the art of verbal manipulation to cover up inadequacies, a danger exists. The danger of identifying with the aggressor. In the early 1940's, psychologist Bruno Bettleheim was interned in a Nazi concentration camp. There he observed a curious phenomenon. Prisoners began to steal food, inform on their fellows, and ape the goose-stepping stance of their tormentors. Identification with the aggressor predisposes abused children to grow up and abuse their children, which we call the "battered child syndrome." Related to this is the "battering child syndrome" where an abused child maims or kills a younger brother or sister.

Because of the strong tendency for imitative behavior by young men and women aspiring to a profession, the law profession must take special care to combat unethical practices and isolate those who walk the fine line. Many legal cases present genuine cases of moral dilemma over which the attorney must anguish. In a recent case, a lawyer referred a patient to me who was arrested and had confessed to stealing three pair of shoes from a department store while shopping with her daughter-in-law. I asked her about shoe size in order to test her reality contact. She admitted the stolen shoes were size 7½, and that her own size was 5½. Her daughter-in-law, I discovered, wore size 7½. She then confessed to covering up for her shopping companion who had actually stolen the shoes. She explained that her daughter-in-law was also arrested but the patient agreed to lie to the court to protect her. Since I had the patient's permission to provide a report to her attorney, I discussed this revelation and its likelihood of being true. The attorney lamented this information since he was also hired to represent the daughter-in-law. He ultimately decided to withdraw from both clients because of irreparable conflict of interest.

Unethical practices interestingly account for only 9% of malpractice suits. According to a recent survey, 45% of such suits involve "forgetfulness" such as errors in statute of limitations, missed appearances in court, misfiled documents, etc. Errors in legal judgment are the basis for 25% of malpractice claims and the remaining 21% is accounted for by instances of unclear relationship between clients and lawyers. Not suprisingly, the larger the firm, the more likely is the "forgetfulness" problem, where division of labor is complex and delegation and responsibility includes minutia. In a large Dallas firm, one lawyer's sole corporate responsibility is ordering furniture.

If societal expectations are somehow unreal, expectations of the legal profession for its own members are at least illusive. These expectations are of two types: formal and informal. Chief Justice Arthur Vanderbilt noted five formal attributes typifying the attorney and his role: *counseling advocacy, dedication to improvement of the profession, leadership* and *the unselfish holding of public office.* Most attorneys would theoretically agree that the five attributes represent an ideal toward which behavior would be directed. Counseling suggests scholarship, concern and insight germane to any form of legal practice, but also implies expertise. In divorce actions, counseling regarding the welfare of children is usually indicated. The attorney's energy is more frequently directed toward petitions, restraining orders, property settlement and child support.

In 1970, the Texas Family Code provided for court-appointed counselors upon petition in divorce cases. Counseling is at the court's discretion. Instead of utilizing the opportunity for psychotherapy and crisis intervention many Texas attorneys petition counseling only as a delaying tactic. The Texas Legislature did safeguard against subverting the counseling process. No psychologist-appointed counselor may be a witness for or against either party. Marriage and family counseling by attorneys is a legitimate and desirable activity. A few attorneys abuse this obligation by taking a soap box stand. One senior lawyer of 30 years experience probes the divorce client for other than no-fault grounds, then delivers a scathing lecture on the sanctity of marriage and sends the client home. The California approach requiring pre-marital counseling seems most enlightened. Alvin Toffler, author of *Future Shock,* believes marriages of the future will be successive; that each person will marry several times to meet different needs at different stages of life.

Advocacy, rooted in the adversary process,has always been the medium of trial proof in America for settling disputes and criminal allegations. Although cases at law from a psychological point of view may have two, three or more sides, the attorney by training, is predisposed to hammer the issues into a two-sided model of plaintiff and defendant, or prosecutor and defendant. Exceptions to this are cases involving joinder of several defendants or plaintiffs. More discomforting is the committment to aggression—that like the Roman Gladiator, the lawyer must fight or be destroyed. One trial attorney told me recently, "Clients and jurors like an attorney who is a fighter, a scrapper." This attitude may have questionable validity but reflects history since medieval British law required disputes to be settled by combat, trial by fire and by water.

To be intensively aggressive in court creates tension and stress for the attorney. These two factors, observes the noted physiologist, Selye, contribute to "the aging process." Psychosomatic symptoms of stress such as nausea, migraine headaches and ulcers are the battle scars of trial work. Prolonged chronic stress is a factor in understanding suicide and alcoholism. Yet everybody seems surprised to read in the morning newspaper that a successful attorney had been arrested for driving while intoxicated or has taken his own life. Female lawyers may contribute to changing the aggressiveness ideal in court. Women's movements preach aggressiveness as a value, but female lawyers explained to me that in court they avoid being bellicose. This disarms the male adversary who was raised never to insult, trap, embarrass or be disrespectful to a lady. The wolf becomes a lamb.

For the member of the small law firm or for the vanishing number of sole practitioners who must compete with the large firm lawyer, the strain of preparation is often fatigue. New York, Los Angeles, Chicago and Houston all have firms of over one hundred attorneys which permit one individual to amass in-depth knowledge of a particular area such as corporate law, oil and gas or real estate, and others to specialize mainly in trial work or appellate advocacy. This is often a disadvantage to the young lawyer who seeks broad experience but who may be permitted to rotate through several departments. While small firm lawyers or sole practitioners can also specialize, the economics of practice usually requires them to provide broader services. Many of them prevail in verdicts or judgment over the large firm lawyer, but the amount of time for case preparation is greater and the challenge is more exhausting. Typically, small firm lawyers work longer hours.

Recent law graduates are the neophytes and oppressed members of the bar. The emotional stress can be overwhelming. Here, the young lawyer with a small firm has the advantage since he is usually given greater responsibility, and he has more contact with the partners who control his fate. Freshman members of large firms may never even meet all the partners except at a Christmas party. Martin Mayer, in his book *The Lawyers,*[3] describes a confrontation between a partner and freshman lawyer over the completion date of a certain memorandum. With intimidation, the senior lawyer inquires, "Tell me the truth—that you wanted to go home early Sunday night." Frustrated with low pay and undesirable cases discarded by the senior lawyers, the young lawyer waits until his confidence has peaked and then asks for a raise, percentage of firm profits or even partner status. If the neophyte has brought important clients to the firm or if firm-referred clients will now deal only with him, he makes a good case. Otherwise, he terminates or is asked to resign. Many young lawyers complain to me that they are only hired as cheap labor and that their firms hire and after a period of effort, fire the recent graduate on a regular basis.

Justice Vanderbilt designated leadership and the unselfish holding of office as an attribute of a lawyer. It is ego gratifying to believe that one has special responsibility for community service. The fallacy of leadership is a delusion of the American middle class that children and adolescents must become leaders and never be "average." The story of a young mother filling out an application to send her son to summer camp illustrates the point. When confronted by the question, "Is your child a leader or a follower?", she thought a moment and wrote, "If William is not a leader, I'm certain that he will be a good follower." Some time later, she received a personal response from the Camp Director: "Dear Madam, We are pleased to accept William to camp this summer. Although he is to be the only follower at camp this season, I am certain he will make an excellent adjustment."

Despite or because of this fixation for leadership, lawyers have historically held high public offices disproportionate to their numbers in general population. Since 1900, America has had eleven presidents. No less than nine of them were attorneys or had studied

---

3. Martin Mayer, THE LAWYERS, Dell Publishing Co., New York, 1966.

law: McKinley, Teddy Roosevelt, Taft, Wilson, Coolidge, Franklin Roosevelt, Johnson, Nixon and Ford. One notable exception is Harry Truman, whose biographers describe his early vocation as a **railroad time keeper. From the 71st through the 75th Congress, an average of 68% of the Senators were attorneys and for that** same period, 61% of the House members were lawyers. As I prepared to graduate from law school, one professor had this tongue in cheek advice: "Seek public office when you return home to practice law. It will give you public exposure which the Canons of Ethics otherwise prohibit. Just pray that you don't win."

Few members of the bar find difficulty in accepting Justice Vanderbilt's proposition that a "dedication to improving the profession" is desirable. Yet there is almost no agreement on what this phrase means. Attitudes on this issue vary with geography, the institution of legal training, ethnicity, age, sex, economic security and other psycho-social factors. Should specializations be published in legal directories in the Yellow Pages? Should national law exams be implemented and should law school entrance exams themselves be re-examined? Should group legal services be sanctioned, should trials be videotaped, and should no fault insurance continue to be opposed? Counseling, advocacy, leadership, the unselfish holding of public office and dedication to improving the profession are all formal attributes of professional expectations represented within the attorney's frame of reference, but their poignancy is not as relevant as the societal expectations shared by lawyers—often at the unconscious level. An attorney's attitude toward himself may depend on who his clients are.

Prestige is borrowable. Store clerks at luxurious department stores may show contempt and disgust for customers who are reluctant to buy their most expensive products. The clerk himself could ill afford to do the same. College professors may grow long hair and wear jeans to class. This phenomenon reveals the psychological process of identification. Psychologists identify with their patients, and the attorney identifies with his clients. The attorney who represents Sears, T.W.A., or the biggest bank in town perceives himself as having a more significant impact on the affairs of men than does the attorney who represents the local grocer, hardware store owner or airline mechanic.

Some trial attorneys experience ego gratification at their capacity to confound and discredit an expert witness, such as a physician or psychologist in court. An orthopedic surgeon complained to me recently of a Dallas attorney who grilled him on the stand for three hours about a patient he had only seen for one visit. He begrudgingly admitted respect for the lawyer's skill. The skillful lawyer manipulates expert witness answers via the rules of evidence, by challenging expert opinions with allusions to treatises and by acquiring considerable technical knowledge during case preparation. It is painful but important for the psychologist to prepare for the ordeal and challenge of cross examination by realizing that the attorney has only three purposes—to discredit the doctor's credentials, to discredit the doctor's findings, and to discredit the doctor as a person. Unconsciously, the attorney may enjoy whittling the psysician or psychologist down to size, thereby building his own esteem. The following dialogue illustrates the potential humiliation of a senior psychologist of considerable reputation testifying about his findings of psychosis for a criminal defendant accused of armed robbery based on a diagnostic interview and psychological testing. The prosecution is zeroing in on the testing phase of the examination.

Prosecutor: Now doctor, you testified that as part of your diagnostic interview with the defendant, you administered a series of psychological tests, including the draw a House—Tree—Person test. Is that correct?

Psychologist: Yes.

Prosecutor: Do you know Professor Harvey Kroler and are you familiar with his book entitled, *Psychological Measurement*?

Psychologist: Yes.

Prosecutor: What is the professional reputation of Professor Kroler and of his text?

Psychologist: He is an eminent psychologist who specializes in psychometric diagnostics. His text is adopted in many universities in this country.

Prosecutor: Do you consider Dr. Kroler an expert in diagnosis of mental illness with regard to psychological test instruments?

Psychologist: Yes.

Prosecutor: Well doctor, on page 347 of his text, he states and I quote, "The House—Tree—Person test is of questionable validity as a diagnostic tool." Doctor, you testified that a symptom of the defendant's psychotic depression was that he drew a house with no windows and a tree with no leaves. Is that correct? Please answer yes or no.

Psychologist: Yes, but that is only one index of—

Prosecutor: Please confine your answer to yes or no. Doctor, if one of the men or women on the jury panel drew a house with no windows in it, would you say that they were psychotic or crazy?
*(Jury laughter)*
If His Honor drew a tree with no leaves on it, would you say that it was winter, or that he was mentally ill?

Although the lawyer may gain personal esteem by confounding the expert witness, his own competency is increasingly challenged from within his own profession. Writing for the *Barrister*,[4] A.B.A. President (1974) Chesterfield Smith questions the assumptions that a "license to practice law should be for life" and that lawyers are "omnicompetent to perform all legal tasks." Mr. Smith argues that state bar associations should institute re-licensing procedures based on peer group evaluations and continuing education programs. He also calls for regulated specialization on legal practice. Currently, only patent law is recognized as a speciality.* One problem with the latter suggestion is the practitioner in the small town or rural area

4. C. Smith, "The Case for Periodically Compelling Lawyers to Prove Their Competency," BARRISTER, April, 1974, p. 8
*Several states, including Texas, are preparing to test for specialty competency.

where specialization does not meet community needs. The medical profession dealt with both the desirability of specialization and community needs by recognizing the general practitioner as a specialist in family medicine. If re-licensing is to include re-testing, an interesting Equal Employment Opportunity problem emerges. The Supreme Court in Griggs vs. Duke Power Co. (1971) has held that tests of employment must be job related. The tests are not deemed discriminatory if a relationship can be shown between good job performance and high test scores. It is questionable that lawyers earning high bar exam test scores are the best lawyers or that physicians scoring highest on medical boards are the most effective doctors.

## Specialties in Modern Legal Practice

Admiralty

Agency

Air Law

Anti-Trust

Arbitration

Business Organizations

Commercial Property

Comparative Law

Constitutional Law

Corporations

Corporate Finance

Creditor's Rights

Credit Transactions

Criminal Law

Domestic Relations

Estate Planning

Estates and Trusts

Federal Practice

Government Contracts

Insurance

International Law

Labor Law

Land Use

Law & Medicine

Law & Poverty

Law & Psychology

Legislation

Local Government

Military Law

Mining

Negotiable Instruments

Oil & Gas

Patents, Copyrights & Trademarks

Property

Regulated Industries

Taxation

Torts

Trade Regulation

Water Law

Workman's Compensation

In quest of prestige and academic recognition, American law

schools have shed the LL.B., the Bachelor of Law degree for the J.D., Juris Doctor. The rationale for this change was that most professional law schools require a Bachelors Degree as a requirement for admission to law school, and that the J.D. would reflect graduate training. The point is well taken. Confusion has resulted for the public however, because prior to adopting the J.D., law schools began offering a LL.M. degree, Masters of Law, and also an S.J.D. degree, Doctor of Juridicial Science. In academia, the Masters degree precedes the Doctorate. In law, one acquires a Doctorate before a Masters degree and then has the opportunity to earn a more advanced Doctorate. Nevertheless, the Canon of Ethics discourages lawyers from displaying J.D. after their names or referring to themselves by the title "Dr." because it leads to "self laudation." The real reason for discouraging displaying the degree is that some lawyers don't have one. This group earned their degree through apprenticeship. Prior to the State Bar of Texas examination procedure, a person worked for a lawyer as an apprentice and then when he felt confident, went before a district judge to be examined over equity maxims and his motivation for practicing law.

Prestige is also borrowed from business and social contracts. The contract phenomenon is a ritualistic interaction with others in a barter situation. It can be described as a game. One individual searches out another in the hope that the other will be helpful to him at some future time. It is the quid pro quo tied to a condition subsequent. One cynical lawyer suggested the game could be simplified by a contract list signed by persons meeting one another, dispensing with the insincere friendship and affability. Many law students believe that the success of their practice will be more strongly affected by the nature and number of their contacts than by the quality of their services. Many senior attorneys agree.

Not suprisingly, lawyers who deny and protest the value of contacts, continue to play the game for fear of being outdone by those who do play it. Psychologists call this defense mechanism projection. Projection was illustrated in a psychological study by Professor Sears, who asked 97 fraternity men at a large university to rate each other along the characteristics of stinginess, obstinacy and disorderliness. Individuals rated high by fraternity brothers as being stingy, tended to be those who most frequently saw stinginess in others. C. W. Mills, the noted sociologist observes:

> The young lawyer, just out of law school, fresh from matching wits with law professors and bar examiners, lacks one thing important for successful practice—contacts. Not only knowledge of trade secrets, but the number of contacts, is the fruit of what is called experience in modern business professions. The young men may labor and provide many of the ideas for the produce that goes out under the older man's name, but the older man is the business-getter through his contacts. Karl Llewellyn has observed; "He can attract more orders than he or twenty like him can supply." The measure of such a man is the volume of business he can produce; he creates the job for the young salaried lawyers, then puts his label on the product. He accumulates his reputation outside the office from the success of the young men, themselves striving for admittance to partnership, which comes after each has picked up enough contacts that are too large and dangerous to allow him to be kept within the salaried bracket. In the meantime, he sweats, and in the meantime, the new law school graduates are available every year, making a market with depressed salaries, further shut out by those new young men who have already inherited through their families a name that is of front office caliber. The powerful connection, the strategic marriage, the gilt-edged social life, these are the obvious means of success.
>
> Source: C. W. Mills, WHITE COLLAR, p. 125-6. By permission of Oxford University Press.

If Mills is correct—that a marriage for an attorney can be strategic, then psychologist Dr. Eric Fromm may also have a point when he defines love as the best two individuals can do in the marriage market place considering the worth of salability of their personalities.

The adversary process is structured for competitiveness. In his transactional analysis of the courtroom game, Dr. Eric Berne suggests that the underlying dynamics of competitiveness are in childhood experience, sibling rivalry.[5]   Sigmund Freud,[6] the father of clinical psychology and psychoanalysis, took a more primeval view of competitiveness.   He depicted the genesis of civilization as an effort of a leader or father figure to avoid being killed by younger tribal members who coveted his tools, animals and women.   But we know that competitiveness is not an inborn drive; it is learned.   The Zuni Indians of the Southwest United States illustrate the societal importance of competition.   In Zuni culture, the highest compliment paid to a tribal member was, "Nobody ever heard of you."   In a Zuni school house, the first student to finish a problem at the blackboard did not spin around rapidly, waving his hand in order to receive appropriate reinforcement from the teacher, and assert status superiority.   Rather, he erased and started over in order to avoid the embarrassment of "standing out."   The competition neurosis (fear of being surpassed) is seen in the relations of nations as well as individuals.   The United Nations Treaty on Outer Space adopted in 1967 reveals the paranoid fear that one country will expropriate a celestial body at the expense of another, though there are those who think that the moon should be annexed as the 51st state.

### Biophysical Factors

Biophysical factors emphasize self perception.. How does one perceive himself—personable and handsome, uninteresting or ugly? Self worth, feelings of adequacy and extroversion are determined in part by body image.   The criminologist Lombroso believed that criminal tendencies could be discovered by measuring skull size. Psychologist-physician William Shelton believed that body types correlated with personality traits.   His system is summarized below.

| BODY TYPE | PERSONALITY TYPE |
| --- | --- |
| Endomorphy (heavy, obese) | Viceratonia (fun loving, jovial) |
| Mesomorphy (athletic, verile) | Somatatonia (aggressive, extroverted) |
| Ectomorphy (thin, frail) | Cerebratonia (introversion, lack of confidence) |

5. Eric Berne, GAMES PEOPLE PLAY, Grove Press, New York, 1964.
6. Sigmund Freud, THE BASIC WRITINGS OF SIGMUND FREUD, Random House, 1938.

Researchers Ellen Bersheid, Elaine Walster and George Bohrnstedt surveyed 62,000 readers of the magazine, *Psychology Today*[7] about their body image. They found that only 45% of the women and 55% of the men surveyed were satisfied with their bodies. While the readers were able to express dissatisfaction with particular facial features, especially teeth, complexion or noses, only 11% of the men and 8% of the women expressed dissatisfaction with their faces in general. So compelling is body image, that Professor Stone of the University of Minnesota discovered that people will rehearse themselves physically in front of a mirror before going to an important meeting just as they will rehearse what they are going to say. The researchers concluded that just as Hertz makes Avis try harder, so being unattractive predisposes one to develop compensating attributes such as an interesting personality, scholarship, wealth or power. Dr. Joyce Brothers observed that attractiveness can be traded off in marriage for another desirable attribute; that the brainy guy marries the beautiful girl. As a result, he feels less ugly and she feels more intelligent.

There are numerous examples of individuals whose acute dissatisfaction with their body image, because of unattractiveness or physical handicap, provides the psychic energy for great achievement. The creator of western civilization's most beautiful sculpture, Michelangelo, was grotesque in appearance. The eloquent Greek orator, Demosthenes, suffered from a speech impediment during adolescence. President Theodore Roosevelt, a physical fitness buff, was a frail and sickly child. Moshe Dayan, the charismatic Israeli general, was perceived by his enemies as more mysterious and cunning because of his black eye patch. One successful attorney I know of, elicits great confidence in his clients because he is aggressive and extroverted despite an atrophied right arm. Perhaps the way an attorney appears on television will someday affect his self perception and worth as a trial lawyer. Federal Rule of Criminal Procedure 53 prohibits taking photographs in court. But video taping of a deposition

---

7. Berscheid, Walster & Bohrnstedt, "Body Image," PSYCHOLOGY TODAY, Nov. 1973, p. 119-131.

given by an attorney to a mentally ill person has already been admitted into evidence by a Pennsylvania court.[8]

The successful attorney seeks critical self analysis of his own motivation—why he became a lawyer, why he practices, what he does, where he goes and even why he asks a client or witness a particular question. Psychologist Abraham Maslow conceptualized motivation as existing on a pyramid consisting of tiers:

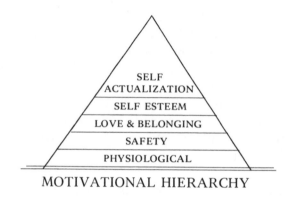

MOTIVATIONAL HIERARCHY

The most basic needs are physiological needs. They are positioned at the base and include thirst, hunger, sex, respiration and sleep. If these needs are not satisfied, man cannot exist. The second tier, "safety," underlies man's need for security and stability in life. Successful attorneys are not gamblers, they are moderate risk takers who consider the safety of their positions. Plea bargaining and the negotiated settlement grow out of an abhorence of the extreme risk and sometimes injustice of "winner takes all." Maslow's third tier represents the motive for love and belonging. Man has a need for sharing meaningful experience through a heterosexual relationship, and to belong to groups, clubs or firms that provide comradeship and shared ideal. The self esteem tier represents a person's need to think well of himself. The highest motive in man, says Maslow, is self actualization—the realization of one's total potentiality. Few achieve this. In Maslow's model, a higher tier cannot be achieved until all tiers below it are achieved.

8. G. Kornblum & P. Rush, "T.V. in Courtroom and Classroom," A.B.A. JOURNAL, March, 1973. pp. 273-274.

In their text on personality theory, Drs. Hall and Lindzey[9] provide fifteen characteristics of the self actualized person:

## Characteristics of Self Actualizing Persons

1. They are realistically oriented.
2. They accept themselves, other people, and the natural world for what they are.
3. They have a great deal of spontaneity.
4. They are problem centered rather than self-centered.
5. They have an air of detachment and a need for privacy.
6. They are autonomous and independent.
7. Their appreciation of people and things is fresh rather than stereotyped.
8. Most of them have had profound mystical or spiritual experiences, although not necessarily religious in character.
9. They identify with mankind.
10. Their intimate relationships with a few specially loved people tend to be profound and deeply emotional rather than superficial.
11. Their attitudes and values are democratic.
12. They do not confuse means with ends.
13. Their sense of humor is philosophical rather than hostile.
14. They have a great fund of creativeness.
15. They resist conformity to culture.

Special insight into the personalities of lawyers can be gleaned from talking to non-attorneys who work side by side with attorneys. In 1972, I made a study of the impressions of legal secretaries on the personalities of their bosses.[10]  In the main, they perceived the attorneys they worked for as being extremely competent. On a 7 point scale (7 being extremely competent), they rated their bosses with an average rating of 6.2. Nevertheless, they perceived some attorneys as procrastinating about important decisions, being disorganized, tending to be moody at the office and lacking motiva-

9. Hall and Lindzey, THEORIES OF PERSONALITY, John Wiley and Sons, New York: 1957. p. 327.
10. Robert Gordon, "We Asked Your Secretary," CASE AND COMMENT, May-June, 1972. pp. 35-37.

tion. In this regard, one secretary verbalized her wish that the boss was more productive on "out of town trips."

While many laymen perceive the attorney as hardnosed and coolly rational, several secretaries noted that their bosses were too forgiving. As one said, "He has a gruff voice, but a soft heart." A surprising number of secretaries suggested that attorneys need to pay more attention to the interpersonal aspects of practice, *i.e.* being sensitive and warm with clients. As one legal secretary put it, "My boss is absorbed and in love with the law. It's only the practice of it that bogs him down." When asked about intra-office flirtations, most reported handling the situation casually or jokingly. The flirtations seldom moved in an intimate direction. "He wouldn't have time," observed one. "Not bothered now," was the response of a 65 year old legal secretary. "I tell him to wait till after dinner," reported another. This last response reflected a marital as well as secretarial relationship.

I asked the secretaries why, in their opinions, attorneys became attorneys. Financial remuneration was mentioned, but not as often as expected. The majority of legal secretaries viewed attorneys as men and women of intelligence, ambition and ego strength who derive enjoyment from helping others. Words like "dedication," "love of the law," "family tradition," "prestige," and "satisfaction in helping" were commonly descriptive. Most revealing is the fact that over 90% of our participants would like a son or daughter of theirs to become an attorney. This is a cogent index of identification. Comments of secretaries included, "I most assuredly would," "I would encourage him in every way," "my son is pre-law," "increasing community need," "a respected profession," "to follow in the footsteps of his grandfather."

In this chapter, the "law is man" theory and its consequences have been explored. The theory maintains that to understand and practice law effectively, one must understand himself and the societal pressures and expectations which shape his personality, attitudes and behavior. This inquiry of self analysis can begin with the deceivingly simple question, "Who am I?" In Chapter II, the assumptions which the attorney internalizes through law school training and experience are scrutinized for their validity and usefulness.

# chapter 2

# Assumptions,
# Presumptions
# and Fact

Montanien 75

# ASSUMPTIONS

Behind the logical form lies a judgment as to the relative worth and importance of competing grounds, often an inarticulate and unconscious judgment it is true, and yet at the very root and nerve of the whole proceeding. You can give any conclusion a logical form. You can always imply a condition in a contract. But why do you imply it? It is because of some belief as to the practice of a community or of a class, or because of some opinion as to policy, or in short, because of some attitude of yours upon a matter not capable of exact quantitative measurement, and therefore not capable of founding exact legal conclusions.

The author of this insight challenges the assumption that law is based on logical thought. He suggests that logic is only a mask for community expectations and unconscious subjective feelings. The passage was written in 1897 before Freud's concept of unconscious determinism of behavior was fully developed by Oliver Wendell Holmes, attorney and jurist.

For some mysterious reason, events which should be explained fully are instead explained away by the not so explanatory phrase, "It's an assumption." The phrase, "it's an assumption" suggests that investigation is not required. Assumptions are a matter of faith. Professor G. M. Stratton challenged the assumptions of our perceptual world by designing prismed goggles which change our visual point of view (left becomes right, up becomes down). At first, an individual who puts on the Stratton goggles experiences disorientation and hand-eye coordination is impaired. His world would appear to swirl. By walking left to avoid bumping into a chair appearing to be on the right, the goggled person bumps right into it. After a period of time however, he is able to function quite well as he learns to live and work in an inverted world. One volunteer who wore the goggles for several hours was asked whether furniture in the room where he stood appeared to be upside down. When his visual assumptions were challenged, he became confused:[11]

> I wish you hadn't asked me. Things were all right until you popped the question to me. Now, when I recall how they did look before I put on the lenses, I must answer that they do look upside down now. But until the moment you asked me, I was absolutely unaware of it and hadn't given a thought to the question of whether things were right side up or upside down.

Professor K. U. Smith, a psychologist at the University of Wisconsin, was able to illustrate the disturbing effects of erroneous assumptions with an audition experiment in which participating college students were asked to don earphones which isolated them from extraneous noises and sounds. The earphones even prevented them from hearing their own voices despite the fact that human voice sounds are partially transmitted through bone structures in the jaw and skull. One assumption challenged by the Smith study was that as each of us speaks, we assume that we hear our own voice instantaneously, and that if any feedback delay exists, it is very slight, so slight that we don't notice it. As each student spoke, Smith fed the student's voice into a computer system which had been programmed to delay at various intervals the time required to return the voice pattern to the earphones of the person who spoke. By increasing the time lapse between speaking and hearing one's voice, a significant number of students began to stutter. Interviewed later, the students reported that they were unaware of any speech or hearing distortions.

The famous analyst Dr. Alfred Adler noted the human tendency to regard assumptions as fact. He called the internalizing of these assumptions "fictional finalisms." Adler believed an understanding of assumptions was indispensable to an understanding of all psychological phenomenon. Thus, if an attorney believes everyone is manipulative and Machiavellian, that everyone has his price, and that anyone would lie to save his own skin, then such beliefs will affect the degree to which he is willing to trust others. If an

---

11. Pronko & Snyder, VISION WITH SPATIAL INVERSION, Wichita, Kansas University Press, 1952.

32

adversary in a negligence case calls and announces, "Don't bother taking Mr. Frank's deposition, we're not going to call him to testify," then the attorney's assumption of trustworthiness of colleagues or of a particular colleague is challenged. Forensic psychologists whose evaluations of patients contribute to case development, also have their assumptions of truthfulness tested. Recently while in therapy with a patient, my secretary buzzed to announce that a court reporter was in the waiting room. The reporter presented a subpoena duces tecum for the file of a child who had fallen off a defective porch of a rented house and sustained injuries to her head which resulted in perceptual and learning problems. The subpoena looked impressive. It recited the court and cause number and the litigants' names. It had a dollar attached and had the reporter's seal affixed. Closer scrutiny revealed that the subpoena did not have the judge's or the judge's clerk's signature. I refused to honor the so-called subpoena.

The attorney assumes that clients come to him because they have legal problems. As we discuss in the following chapter, this is not always the case. What appear to be legal problems are often psychological problems with legal manifestations. Unfortunately, many attorneys have treated them alike. Attorneys also assume that they know what result the client desires. In a child abuse case referred to me, a young couple had their two-year-old daughter removed from their home following the allegation of a downstairs apartment neighbor that they had physically abused their child. Criminal charges were also filed and the attorney was able to bring in a no bill for want of probable cause that abuse had occurred. The father maintained that on two occasions his son had fallen from a table, which resulted in a broken rib and arm. A county physician testified that the differential in healing indicated abuse. Following the grand jury's no bill, the attorney petitioned the court for the child's return. As time approached for the custody hearing, the father became increasingly uncooperative, which the attorney interpreted as lack of gratitude. I showed the attorney a picture which the father had drawn of himself, his wife and his daughter at my request. The picture, shown right, shattered the attorney's assumption that once acquitted of child abuse, a father would naturally want the return of the child.

Legal training and experience elicit an assumption that law has a compelling, salient and poignant effect on society. So generic is this assumption, that it is never challenged. Can it be properly tested? A simple experiment will suffice. Take two major urban areas matched for population, variation in culture and the literacy of its inhabitants. Then suspend all law in one for 24 hours; observe and measure effects in both cities. Would the city without law destroy itself, would there be widespread murder, theft and rape? Would businessmen break contracts? Would partners disavow their liability, would trustees invade trust corpus? We might infer what would occur in the experiment by studying data on cities where police strikes have taken place, such as Boston and Montreal, Canada. There is, of course, a difference between suspending law and suspending law enforcement. No appreciable increase in crime was reported during the strikes.

We know that when a stop light is removed from an intersection where motorists are accustomed to seeing it or when it isn't functioning properly, the behavior of drivers is still conforming. Most drivers will stop either out of habit, caution or guilt. The unequivocal assumption that all behavior in a city without formal law would become antisocial, criminal or tortuous is not warranted.

Some patterns of human activity would not change at all. Where strong and compelling norms exist, breaking the norms could lead to more punishing consequences than breaking the law. For example, though murder would be legal for 24 hours, members of society would still believe murder undesirable, and resort to social ostracism or even vigilante groups to remedy what they considered to be evil.

The practicing attorney assumes that every man and woman has free will; that each individual is captain of his ship, and to a great extent determines the nature of his future. Free will implies that an individual has the freedom to contract and the freedom, but not the right, to break a contract. It implies that an automobile collision which could have been avoided, occurred because one or both parties were negligent. It implies that a man dies intestate because he freely chose to do so. According to free will theory, an assault and battery, a defamation, or a theft are committed because the defendant intended the act and accomplished it by his own volition as a consequence of the intent.

If a death is shown to be "accidental," the defendant is acquitted. If an auto injury is found to be the result of an "unavoidable accident" the defendant is not liable. But what is an accident, and why does the law hold individuals less responsible for them? Freud believed accidents did not exist as such and that they were purposeful and reflected unconscious motivation. It is estimated that 40% of all automobile accidents involve suicidal or homicidal acting out. Freud observed that when we are on the roof of a tall building and look down, we are not so much afraid of falling as we are of jumping. Psychoanalytic theory also suggests that mistakes can be purposeful. Texas Penal Code Article 8.02 states that if an individual, through a mistake, forms a reasonable belief about a fact, this mistaken belief can negate criminal culpability. But this same individual could be convicted of a lesser offense which he would be guilty of if the mistaken belief were actually true. Mistakes in speech or slips of the tongue often reveal true feelings. One colleague recalled the occasion when a patient, suspicious of the psychologist's desire to help him asked, "Are you a fraudian?" That isn't to say things are never as they appear. Once Freud was puffing on a cigar when a colleague reproached the analyst for revealing oral childhood desires for gratification. Freud, it is told, took a deep puff and observed, "My friend, sometimes a cigar is just a cigar."

Free will is the central tenet on which punishment in criminal law and punitive damages in tort are based. If a defendant has no freedom of choice, if we view him as totally manipulated by his circumstances, his physiology and his personality, what right have we to punish him? If we view an automobile accident as the product of factors beyond one's control, what possible basis could there be for liability. Liability is another word for responsibility. Legislators are beginning to change their attitude toward the free will assumption. Non-fault recoveries are provided for in workmen's compensation and in divorce cases. No-fault auto insurance is currently under Congressional scrutiny. Prior to the no-fault ground of personality incompatibility, divorce litigants had to prove adultery, cruelty, sterility, abandonment and desertion as a basis for divorce. No longer must husband and wife agree to catch one another in an extra-marital affair or make public impotency or frigidity. Under workmen's compensation, a pressman who looses an arm doesn't have to prove his company was negligent in maintaining equipment in order to recover. The company is required to meet its responsibility to employees by paying insurance premiums and there is no need for the defense of assumed risk, *e.g.*, that if you're going to be a pressman, you have to assume the risk of an arm injury.

In contrast to law, science is grounded in a radically different assumption. Science assumes that all events and behavior are determined by physiological, personality and environmental factors. It posits that these factors can be measured and that prediction is possible. Let P = personality, X = physiology, and E = environment. Science assumes that we can identify and measure factors P, X and E and then can predict what an individual with a particular P and X will do in a given E. This approach is called "determinism." The free will approach would posit that prediction in the PxXxE situation is impossible since the individual has the freedom to act in a variety of ways.

As the law is inconsistent, also is psychology inconsistent. Psychology as a science maintains a strict deterministic view for research purposes, and then does an about face in psychotherapy, the process of treating patients. If a patient's behavior is determined by factors X, P and E etc., how can the psychologist help the individual adjust to new situations more successfully? The patient's fate would be sealed. But in treating patients psychologists assume free will, that despite childhood and adolescent experience and physical and environmental factors, a patient can change, grow and be effective.

## THE ULTIMATE AUTHORITY DOCTRINE

Authority in law, contrary to the layman's view, is not deposited with the juries, who are the triers of fact or the trial judge who rules on law and procedure; rather it lies with appellate judges, with State Supreme Court Justices or with United States Supreme Court Justices. Ultimate authority is the affirming, reversing or modifying of a lower court's judgment. In a particular case, authority may reside with the skills and judgment of a State Supreme Court Law Clerk. The law clerk is usually a recent law graduate of distinction who serves a one year tenure as a State Supreme Court Justice's Assistant. In some jurisdictions, the law clerk's opinion weighs heavily on the question as to whether a writ will be granted for the Court to hear a case on appeal.

Although one United States Supreme Court Justice recently noted that "interpretation of the constitution should not change with every change in political winds," no one doubts that it does. In 1970, President Nixon's ability to name Justices Burger and Blackman to the High Court, suggested an authority more cogent than the Court itself. This authority risks dissipation to the extent that a president is unable to predict the attitudes of his appointments once they feel secure from impeachment, salary cuts and firing during periods of good behavior. Ironically, it was the Burger Court which in 1974 voted unanimously to require President Nixon to honor the subpoena of Special Prosecutor Leon Jaworski for tapes of presidential conversations. Ironically, the revelation of these tapes which toppled an administration was revealed by an obscure White House Aide, Alexander Butterfield.

Legal authority has artificial limits which take jurisdictional form. Jurisdiction within a state is broken down geographically, as is jurisdiction between states. States have developed different laws regarding identical behavior patterns which raise questions of fairness. One may marry a first cousin in one state, but not in another. A plaintiff may recover in one state in a personal injury case though he was himself negligent to some degree (comparative negligence), but not in another (contributory negligence). Nevertheless, states are slow to adopt uniform laws. Science repudiates geographical limits. It is bordered by experimental controls and by cautious inference made from raw data. But this caution and control often limit the usefulness of information because it is so qualified. For example, the attorney preparing for a drug possession and use case may be chagrined when the psychologist explains that his research with white college students at the University of Texas who come from upper middle class homes, indicates that smoking marijuana does not significantly lead to the use of more toxic drugs within the first six months. This information may become useless under cross examination in a case of a black female who grew up in a decaying urban neighborhood.

The leather bound volumes of law have a charisma of their own. The attorney deftly prepares his case by ferreting out facts, searching the digest, and shepherdizing the reporter system in an effort to trace authority on particular questions. A legal issue may have its genesis in a street fight, a lost warehouse receipt or on the operating table, but the ultimate answer appears to be somewhere in the leather bound volumes. The process of legal research is an attempt to fit facts into categories of earlier holdings. Stare decisis. the relation back to earlier law, encourages rigidity because it implies that the law is law because the leather bound volumes say it's so. Rigidity in law, so often criticized by pensive jurists and the general community, is classically illustrated in Harrington vs. Taylor:[12]

Harrington sued Taylor for damages resulting from his hand being mutilated. Taylor had beaten his wife who, fearing another beating, took refuge in Harrington's house. The follow-

12. HARRINGTON vs. TAYLOR, 36, S. E. 2nd, 227.

ing day, Taylor entered the house and assaulted his wife a second time. The defendant's wife struck him to the ground with an axe and was about to decapitate him when Harrington intervened, caught the axe as it was descending, suffering a badly lacerated hand in the process. In a moment of gratitude, Taylor orally promised to pay Harrington for his injury; but after making a small payment, he refused to pay more.

The Supreme Court of North Carolina held: "The question presented is whether there was a consideration recognized by our law sufficient to support the promise. The Court is of the opinion that, however much the defendant should be impelled by common gratitude to alleviate the plaintiff's misfortune, a humanitarian act of this kind voluntarily performed, is not such consideration as would entitle him to recover at law."

The Court applied "the law" rigorously and accurately for earlier authority clearly supported the position that acts of humanity would not be sufficient consideration to support a contract. In so holding, the North Carolina Court misconstrued the evolution of law, the purpose of law and the meaning of justice. Every attorney knows that justice is not done in every case; and at times, assumes that justice and legal outcomes are not isomorphic, but at times, contradict each other. Although couched in the assumption of prior authority, was the result in Harrington necessary? Consider a 1917 New York case of Wood vs. Lady Duff-Gordon:[13]

Lady Duff-Gordon was a creator of fashions whose certification of dresses reaped huge profits for manufacturers. Wood proposed to turn this ability into profits by having the exclusive right to place her endorsements on the designs of others. She was to have ½ of all profits. Instead of maintaining the exclusive relationship, the defendant endorsed other garments and fabrics without Wood's knowledge or benefit. The agreement was in writing. Lady Duff-Gordon argued that no contract existed because the plaintiff didn't bind himself to anything, *i.e.* no consideration, that he did not promise to use

---

13. Wood vs. Lucy, Lady Duff-Gordon.  118 N. E. 214

reasonable efforts to place her endorsements or market her designs.

The New York appellate court with three dissenting opinions held: "She says the plaintiff does not bind himself to anything. It is true that he does not promise in so many words that he will use reasonable efforts to place the defendant's endorsements and market her designs. We think however, that such a promise is fairly to be implied. The law has out-grown its primitive state of formalism when the precise word was the sovereign talisman, and every slip was fatal. It takes a broader view today. A promise may be lacking and yet the whole writing may be instinct with an obligation imperfectly expressed."

The difference between Harrington and Lady Duff-Gordon is essentially this: the former followed authority to an unjust finding, but the New York Court refused to do the same. It groped, searched, and in reality manipulated statutory language and case law in an effort to realize justice. The great attorney is not preoccupied with *stare decisis;* he recognizes it, is aware of and appreciates it. He utilizes it as a base line from which to depart. He gropes for a theory, a concept, an idea to contribute to a change in court orientation. He is unwilling to pursue *stare decisis* to an unsuccessful outcome for his client. Preoccupation with *stare decisis* is a distinction between the legal technician and the effective attorney. The technician listens to his client's problem, and if the client's position is contrary to precedent, he sends the client home with a treatise-like lecture on the law. The effective attorney under similar circumstances explains the law, but tells the client further research is needed to see if the client's position can be distinguished from the law or if there is an opportunity to change the court's view of things.

The whole field of equity developed because it became clear that following authority did not always lead to just holdings. Thus developed the maxims of equity. Equity will not suffer a wrong without a remedy, equity aids the vigilant, equity follows the law, equity will only help those with clean hands. This last maxim is illustrated by a Texas case of the 1920's when the Ku Klux Klan sued another organization similarly engaged in intimidating Blacks, Jews and Catholics. The Klan sought equitable relief including injunction against the group using a name deceptively similar to their own. The Court recognized the legal rights of organizations such as the Klan, but refused to grant relief under the equity maxim, "equity will not help those with dirty hands."

Jurists Louis Brandeis and Samuel Warren recognized the rigidity of law in viewing all rights as property rights and argued brilliantly, and in retrospect successfully, for the recognition of rights in personality. This was the forerunner of protection of individual rights such as privacy and freedom from mental distress:

> We must therefore conclude that rights so protected, whatever their exact nature, are not rights arising from contract or from special trust, but are rights as against the world . . . the principle which has been applied to protect these rights is in reality not the principle of private property, unless that word be used in an extended and unusual sense. The principle, which protects personal writings and any other productions of the intellect or of the emotions, is the right to privacy, and the law has no new principle to formulate when it extends this protection to the personal appearance, sayings, acts and to personal relation, domestic or otherwise.[14]

It took nearly 80 years for a court of jurisdiction to agree with Warren and Brandeis. The Senate Watergate hearings of 1974 revealed wire taps, tape recordings of private conversations and Internal Revenue investigations without legitimate national security concerns having been raised. In 1970 Daniel Eisenberg wrote a telling indictment of lost privacy in a technological society. The founder of Tracers Company of America, Eisenberg penned an article entitled "If You Plan to Disappear."[15] In it he argued that while we cherish the naive notion that we could disappear in society if we really wanted to, the odds were 100 to 1 against our succeeding because of records compiled on each of us, our appear-

---

14. 4 HARVARD REVIEW, 213
15. D. Eisenberg, "If You Plan to Disappear", Nov.-Dec. 1970, CASE AND COMMENT.

ance, family background and habits. To establish the right to privacy at law, creative lawyers did not rest on *stare decisis* which said that privacy rights did not exist or that if they did, privacy was only recognized when connected to another right such as property. One approach taken to change the court's position was to seek out custom previously thought irrelevant or inconsequential, and revitalize it. U.S. Senator Sam Erwin illustrated this approach by arguing the right of privacy could be based on a common law concept centuries old — that even the King of England could not enter the cottage of his most humble subject without permission.

A second approach to changing a court's legislative position is reapplication of an already accepted concept. Elland Archer, City Attorney of Mesquite, Texas, took on the Bell Telephone System over the issue of the unsolicited telephone call. Ma Bell had maintained that such calls couldn't be regulated and that in any event, she was not responsible for them since the telephone in a private home is a "privilege" she granted to customers. Archer argued pursuasively for a regulatory ordinance that prescribed daytime hours for business calls to private homes and excluded evenings and Sundays. Each merchant calling homes would have to identify himself with a number and any violation was a misdemeanor. To find a legal basis for the resolution of a community problem, he argued that if the telephone in a residence was a privilege, it was a privilege granted to the Bell System by the customer through a city franchise. Secondly, he argued that the unsolicited call was an "electrical trespass" onto an individual's property for which the caller might be liable for damages.

Apparently not everybody is entitled to privacy consideration. Jackie Kennedy Onassis sought relief in a New York Federal District Court to enjoin photographer Ronald Gallaleh from harassing her by snapping her photo wherever she and her children went. Because Mrs. Onassis is a public figure and because the Court was concerned about First Amendment freedoms of the press, it did not require the photographer to cease and desist, but did enjoin him to keep his distance.

Professor Prosser in his treatise, "The Law of Torts",[16] maintains that when the new tort of intentional infliction of mental distress becomes recognized, most privacy cases will be absorbed into it.  At common law, the law was clear—there was no recovery for mental distress.  For example, in Wilkinson vs. Downton,[17] when the defendant played a prank by informing a woman that her husband was in an accident and entreated her to go to the scene for rescue, the court denied recovery.  But exceptions to the no recovery rule were established by persistent trial lawyers who whittled away at precedent.  Courts began to permit recovery for harassment of debtor, failure to deliver a telegram and insults by an employee of a hotel.  No recovery was permitted for mental distress arising from inviting a woman to engage in illicit sexual activity.  The courts apparently adopted a "no harm in asking" attitude regarding this question.

More recently, courts have begun to recognize recovery for mental distress where there is also a physical injury.  Someday, a creative lawyer will persuade the court to recognize mental distress without reference to physical injury.  He may succeed by arguing that whenever a person is distressed, physiological changes in the human body take place.  Universities and university professors who engage in psychological research which includes experimentally eliciting stress in study participants, may be liable.  For example, Professor Berkum and associates took subjects on an airplane ride in order to study stress reactions.  During the flight, the pilot deliberately flew into a storm and then simulated engine trouble, deceiving the passengers into believing the plane would crash.[18]  In the notorious Milgram study, Nazi-like reactions to authority were studied.  Research subjects were asked to aid in an experiment to determine the effect of electricity on learning.  They were exhorted to increase the amount of electric shock administered to an individual who was actually a confederate of the professor and not of course receiving electric current.  Although the confederate pounded the walls and feigned unconsciousness, the subjects were encouraged to continue giving the "victim" larger doses of electricity.

---

16. W. Prosser, THE LAW OF TORTS, West Publishing Co., 1955, p. 643.
17. WILKINSON vs. DOWNTON, 2 Q. B. 57.
18. S. Milgram, BEHAVIORAL STUDIES OF OBEDIENCE, Journal of Abnormal and Social Psychology, 1963, p. 371.

## PRESUMPTIONS AND FACTS

A presumption is an inference that a fact exists although it is not known for certain. Its existence may be inferred because a second fact is proven to exist. At law a presumption may be disputed, but the burden of disputing the inference falls on the challenger. This is often difficult or impossible. In such cases, the erroneous presumption is accepted. In criminal law, an individual is presumed to intend to consequences of his act. If a man illegally enters a house at night and leaves the house with a television set belonging to the owner of the house, the intention to steal the T.V. can be inferred. If the same man enters the house with the intention of stealing the T.V. and once inside, is confronted by the owner and in a state of panic kills him, his intent to steal is "transferred" to the murder. The presumption of "intent" is the edge given to the prosecutor.

Since most convictions require an illegal act and criminal intent, the prosecutor's burden is lightened. Law abiding men and women make scores of presumptions each day, most of which are later proven true. Law breakers also make presumptions which when untrue lead to their discovery and apprehension. Clifford Irving, author of a fake autobiography of the recluse billionaire Howard Hughes, bilked the Time-Life Publishing House out of several hundred thousand dollars. He freely admitted that a faulty presumption was his undoing. He presumed Howard Hughes would not deny the validity of the fake autobiography, and that if he did, the public wouldn't believe him.[19]

The presumption that "every citizen knows the law" is a ludicrous presumption since even jurists with a photographic memory refresh themselves on the law and are frustrated by a yearly avalanche of new decisions and statutes even in a highly specialized field of interest. The purpose of this presumption is to eliminate a defense at criminal law. For example, a defendant who has committed a crime such as tax evasion or who fraudulently sells securities, cannot defend himself by stating, "I admit doing the act, but I didn't know it was illegal."

19. M. Brown, SCENE MAGAZINE, September 29, 1974, pp. 22-24

Full knowledge of the law and its applications is simply not possible. Forming and running bank holding companies are examples. The laws regulating banks are so comprehensive and extensive that several bank presidents have admitted to me that if the Justice Department or their State Banking Commissions wanted to find "something wrong or illegal" with their institutional operations they could, despite all good faith efforts at compliance. The same holds true for corporations with more than 50 employees who attempt to comply with E.E.O.C., O.F.C.C. and Occupational Health and Safety Act regulations.

Every man, woman and child is presumed to be sane. Yet this characteristic is more accurately described as a goal than as a norm. In most states, the defendant can rebut the sanity presumption. In Texas he must show that at the time of the commission of the offense, he did not know that his conduct was wrong or was incapable of conforming his conduct to the requirements of law.[20] Under Texas law, the presumption of insanity can be rebuted before the trial in which case the defendant, if found insane, is committed to a state hospital until rehabilitated. Then he stands trial. Or the defendant may be found insane after conviction but before sentencing, or during appeal of a conviction. All proceedings are stayed until his sanity is restored.[21] In an Oklahoma case, the defendant was convicted of murder, which at that time carried the death penalty by electrocution. He was found insane and committed to the state mental hospital where he was curiously treated with electro-shock therapy.

The effective attorney has sufficient knowledge of psychology to realize that although a client may appear normal on the surface, he may nevertheless be suffering from an emotional disorder which would form the basis of an insanity defense. In a recent case, an attorney whose client was accused of shop-lifting asked me to evaluate her because he suspected she was mentally ill despite the fact that she was able to communicate with him in preparation of her defense and appeared lucid and rational. Following is a summary of her psychological evaluation submitted to the lawyer and finally to the court:

20. Texas Penal Code, Section 8.01
21. Texas Code of Criminal Procedure, Article 46.02

## Psychological Report Summary

The patient is a 26-year-old female held at the Grayson County Jail, charged with the offense of shoplifting. She was the only female in a family of ten children. The patient has three children of her own, all illegitimate. Her first child was born when she was in the 8th grade and she never returned to school. The father of her first child was killed in a gun battle with police officers. Her own father abused her mother physically and abandoned the family when the patient was 15 years old.

Orientation for space and time is within normal limits and her intellectual functioning is borderline normal. She exhibits a passive personality superimposed on a depressed and regressed schizophrenia. Psychopathic and acting out behavior is characteristic of her life style.

For the past six years, she has been a prostitute which emphasizes her hatred of men and her own confused sex role. She reports that her husband, now in prison, tortured her by "putting cigars out on her chest, sexually abused her with coke bottles and beat her with coat hangers." As a child, she was fondled by her older brothers and has had homosexual experiences at the jail.

Over the past several years, she has been habituated to drugs including heroin and cocaine. She reports being on drugs during her shoplifting episode and this may have supported her behavior at that time. Even without drugs, she is subject to breaks in reasoning and judgment. For example, in response to the question, "What would you do if you were the first person in a theater to smell smoke and see fire?" she answered, "To tell you the truth, I wouldn't care if it burned. I'd just try to get out of there."

The patient reports having been incarcerated at Terrell State Hospital at Terrell, Texas. She states that she was committed following a suicide attempt. She is not suicidal presently. According to the patient, the **Terrell** hospital placed her in a half way house program from which she eloped without medical discharge.

An individual is presumed competent to enter into a contractual relationship for the purchase of a house, to enter into a marital agreement and to write a will. Like insanity, the competency presumption can be rebutted to render a marriage void, or a contract voidable. Under the Texas Probate Code, a jury finding that the decedent was of unsound mind can invalidate his will. A person with unsound mind is defined as one who is incompetent to care for himself or manage his property and financial affairs. Several years ago, a young couple who feared that their grandmother's will would be contested on the grounds of competency by a greedy relative and would-be heir, asked me to conduct a psychological evaluation of the elderly lady at the time she composed her will. I found her to have some memory loss for the recent past, but she was generally alert and competent under the legal definition. My report is on file in the event her will is contested at the time of probate.

Competency is a requirement when a patient gives a physician permission to perform surgery. Recent case law suggests that the patient's consent is not sufficient unless he is apprised of dangers inherent in the operation. Some time ago, a surgeon called to request that I help with a 65-year-old female patient whose left leg was gangrenous, and in the doctor's opinion, required amputation within 48 hours. The patient refused surgery. He explained that the patient was mentally ill and incompetent and inquired whether a guardian might be appointed based on a psychological evaluation who could give permission. I explained that if the evaluation concurred with his judgment, a guardianship procedure could achieve the result he sought. The next morning, I received a call from the doctor saying that the patient had just given her consent to surgery and that he was scrubbing in five minutes. The surgeon, whose only interest was to save the woman's life, became perplexed and silent when I explained that if the patient was incompetent to withhold her consent she might also be incompetent to give it.

Property and contract issues and personal injury litigation cases often hinge on a simple but deceiving legal test. In order to prove a defendant negligent, it must be shown in court that he failed to act as a reasonable, prudent person would under the same or similar circumstances. The defendant may try to bar recovery by proving that the plaintiff contributed to his injury by not acting in a reasonably prudent manner. Assume that a man sues a department store because his foot was mangled in the store escalator which he asserts was defective. The store admits the defect, but inquires would a reasonably prudent man look before hopping on and realize the danger? Let's consider other examples. Would a reasonably prudent man seek a legal opinion of an abstract in addition to a title company's guarantee? Would a reasonably prudent man anticipate that a moving firm would not deliver goods across country in three weeks as promised? *Black's Law Dictionary* defines reasonable as *"just and proper, ordinary or usual, having the faculty of reason, ration, governed by reason. . ."* The phrase lacks specificity. Would a reasonably prudent man behave identically to reasonably prudent woman? Would a reasonably prudent five-year-old respond identically to his 55-year-old counterpart? In a suit against parents of student protestors for damages done by the students to university property, could the concept of a reasonably prudent *"radical"* under *"riot conditions"* be tenable, or would the court project its own view with the predictable conclusion that a reasonably prudent student would not become a radical or ever become involved in a riot. The possibility of a reasonably prudent schizophrenic is indeed titillating.

The reasonably prudent man concept presupposes that man is after all—reasonably prudent. This itself is of questionable validity. Freud was deeply disturbed by the basic irrationality of man and postulated the *Id,* a hypothetical personality structure, as the primary source of all tension and energy for human experience. The *Id* is considered to be primitive and instinctual, and includes the *thanatos,* or death wish. The *Id* functions according to the hedonistic pleasure principle—immediate gratification of all wishes either by actual gratification or by wishing or dreaming. If the *Id* had its way, a man motivated to relieve aggressive impulses through violence would proceed to do so without regard to the sex or size of his victim or to his chances of being caught and punished.

The fact that other personality functions repress the desire to fight or displace it in the form of sports or verbal sarcasm does not imply that man is basically rational. Even well adjusted individuals fear the breakthrough of irrational tendencies which they consciously want to control.

In the American system, personal injury cases account for the highest percentage of litigation. Elements necessary for recovery are: the defendant owes the plaintiff a legal duty not to act negligently, that the negligence proximately caused the injury and that damages accrued. The element "proximate cause," like the reasonably prudent man concept, is amenable to psychological scrutiny. The term's meaning relates to causality as understood at law. In the *Polemis* case, a plank was dropped into the hold of a ship producing a spark which exploded petrol vapor, destroying the vessel and its cargo. Judge Scrutton opined that dropping the plank was negligent and that the plaintiff was liable for the proximate results. Later, American courts found it necessary to set limits on responsibility for proximate results, so that if A causes event B, which causes event C, which in turn causes event D, which causes E, A may not be liable for E. Justice Cardozo made this point in the *Palsgraf* case.[22]

Plaintiff was standing on a platform of the defendant's railroad. Running to catch a train, a man carrying a package jumped unsteadily aboard. A doorway guard and a platform guard helped the man on, but in the process of so doing, his package, covered with newspaper, fell into the rails. The package actually contained fireworks which exploded, and the shock which it produced caused scales at the opposite end of the platform to fall. Plaintiff was injured by the falling scales.

The lower court found for the plaintiff, but the higher court reversed. Cardozo explained: "One who jostles his neighbor in a crowd does not invade the rights of others standing at the outer fringe when the unintended contact casts a bomb upon

22. 248 N. Y. 339, 162 N. E. 99.

the ground. The wrongdoer is to them as the man who carries the bomb, not the one who explodes it without suspicion of danger. Life will have to be made over, and human nature transformed before a provision so extravagant can be accepted as the norm of conduct, and the customary standard to which behavior must conform."

We strike a match and fire erupts. Did striking the match cause the fire, or were the two events only related in time and space? Or was the fire caused by a number of variables each insufficient by itself but sufficient in combination with each other, such as chemical composition of match, atmosphere, temperature, wind velocity, illumination, heat and friction? Not too long ago, an article appeared in the **Wall Street Journal** announcing that a relationship had been found between skirt lengths and stock market prices. The author buttressed his argument with impressive statistics supporting the relationship. Did hemlines cause the stock prices to soar? Or were both factors caused by still other factors, namely, a booming economy, cultural feelings of optimism and general prosperity. Stock market experts often take advantage of the general public's misunderstanding of cause and effect relationships with such statements as, "Market soars on rumors of new peace initiative." (Market actually rose 10 points). "Market down because too few investors put faith in yesterday's peace rumor." (Market down a few points). One distinguished market analyst commenting in the **Wall Street Journal** had the great insight to predict, "The market will hold steady over the next few days, but if it doesn't, it will probably break out on one side or the other."

A simple psychological experiment dramatically illustrates the fallacy of imputing cause and effect where none exists. A square and circle are projected on an ordinary movie screen. Both figures move across the screen from left to right, except that the square moves at a faster rate than the circle. What do people see? The most common reaction is, "Oh, that was a movie of a square chasing a circle." Was it really? Let the square touch or superimpose itself on the circle repeatedly and people will see the square "attacking or eating the circle."

The effective attorney attempts to construe reality as accurately as possible. He is skeptical of assumptions and understands the superficiality of presumptions. *Stare decisis* and procedural points are viewed as rules subject to change, for judges and jurymen are flexible enough to suspend the rules, or change the rules when they are persuaded that a larger value is being lost. The effective attorney understands that there are no such things as "facts," there are only probabilities that some event was more or less likely to have occurred. After viewing legal assumptions and presumptions more realistically, the attorney acquires a vantage point for understanding his clients and their emotional needs.

# chapter 3

# Attorney-Client
# Rapport

Montanez 75

Recently a young attorney wrote the author as part of a friendly correspondence discussing the subject of the inter-relationship of psychology and law. Permission was granted to publish a sample of his interesting remarks:

The trouble with much psychological writing on law is that it focuses on irrelevancies. When a client comes to see me, I can't take time to find out whether he has an oedipal complex or whether he loves his mother. I wouldn't know how anyway. I am trained to solve legal questions. I have to decide what category or categories a client's problem falls into, whether he has a case or not, and how to advise him. Depositions may be necessary, witnesses located, pleadings filed and I need to begin concentrating on what kind of evidence and instructions are involved in the event of a jury trial. The client needs to sign a contract for legal services.

From divorce cases, I know some clients are willing to stay all day to discuss their social problems if I let them. The client is paying me to advise him. It's like football. He's handing off his case to me and expects me to run with it - for a touchdown. His first impression of me is very important. If I am not bright and confident, he can walk out of the office and be with another attorney an hour later. Please don't misunderstand. I am concerned about my client's psychological problems. Many attorneys become calloused to client's personal problems after several years of practice. I disagree with them. But as far as why the client is in my office, legal issues take foremost priority.

The attorney graduated from a well-known and respected ivy league law school. Before graduation, he received handsome offers from several well-established firms. He is active in his state bar, takes an interest in civic affairs, and has not begrudged his share of court-appointed cases after building his practice. He is earning the respect of his community, a burgeoning suburb adjacent to a large metropolitan area. He is sympathetic to the "law as law" view discussed earlier, and his comments suggest he is dedicated to deftly applying appropriate law to his clients' cases. In his comments, he alluded to himself 21 times, to the law 16 times, but to his clients only 9 times, as displayed in the graph below.

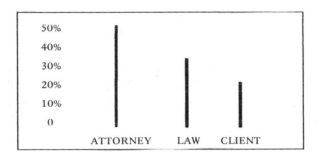

## LETTER REFERENCES

The letter reveals an unfortunate distortion in the traditional legal process which presents the client as an almost extraneous or tangential factor in the legal problem solving equation. In this context, the client becomes depersonalized. He is the defendant, the plaintiff, the respondent or appellant. It is unlikely that he perceives himself in this way. The case docket and reporter system include the client's name in the case style, but after that, case opinions ignore his feelings, his aspirations, and his life style, which are relegated to an inconsequential level. They are instead replaced by the opinioning judge's thoughts on points of law. A case decision is ideographic because it deals with a single individual or with several individuals joined in a single cause of action; but the legal result is nomenthetic, i. e., to be generalized to all persons in like circumstances. While necessary for developing precedent, this procedure is alienating to the client. In court, litigants occupy relatively unimportant spatial positions. The judge sits on an elevated chair protected by an imposing wooden bench. The witness chair and jury's box are also elevated and surrounded by a protective bannister, and even counsels occupy seats more accessible to the aisles.

## THE MOST IMPORTANT PERSON IN THE WORLD

How does the client view his role in the legal process. Does he see himself as a mere cog in the wheel, as part of the courtroom architecture? One industrial psychological study gives us insight into how the client may view himself. White collar workers in a manufacturing plant were asked to diagram their office and to reflect work flow on the pretext that the diagram would reveal their drawing abilities. One office under study included 11 persons: a district manager, three assistants, two executive secretaries, and five office secretaries. Company policy required an organizational flow chart, representing responsibilities and direction of work productivity, to be implemented by the district manager, but it was not made available to others in the office. The organizational flow chart is shown below.

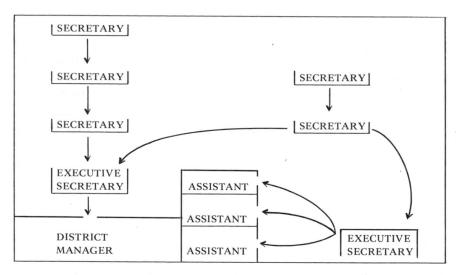

COMPANY ORGANIZATIONAL FLOW CHART

Not surprisingly, the organizational flow chart provided by the company did not even remotely resemble the individual office worker's perception of organizational flow. The following diagram is typical of a secretary's response. Her actual responsibility involved reporting to an executive secretary.

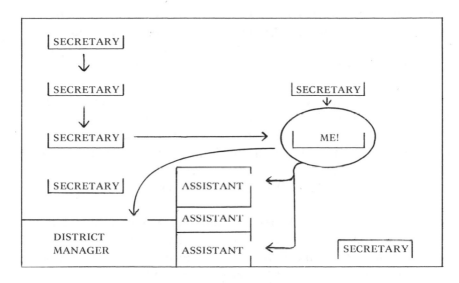

SECRETARY'S PERCEPTION OF ORGANIZATIONAL FLOW CHART

The secretary extended floor space, reduced and increased the size of offices, and dramatically changed the objective nature of organizational responsibility by unconsciously distorting her importance in the scheme of things. In her perception, she related to the assistant managers and to the executive secretary of the district manager. Assistant 2 who she apparently did not perceive herself as relating to, is placed in a smaller office. Most significant is her place in the diagram - she is at the center.

Clients don't think of themselves as clients, or cases, or files, but as terribly important persons with problems involving legal issues or consequences, which motivate them to seek professional help. The most salient dimension of the client's interaction with the law is not winning a case, being acquitted or gaining a $100,000 judgment; it is his feelings of self worth, his perception of fair play, and the quality of his experience with the legal process, and his lawyer. A man convicted and sentenced to five years in a penitentiary for a third offense of theft, feels differently when he believes the judge was impartial, the jury was fair, and his attorney was competent and cared what happened to him, than one who thinks he was abused. Although many incarcerated felons maintain they are innocent, it is imprudent to categorize men and their affairs into the superficial categories of winners and losers.

Certain diagnostic types of clients are easily recognizable by the practicing attorney. The psycholegal syndromes were developed by the author with the collaboration of Dr. Jose Clemente Vivanco of Miami Beach, Florida, as the beginning of a useful classification.

## PSYCHOLEGAL SYNDROMES

*Legophobic reaction:* A neurotic anxiety reaction of some sole proprietors and business executives who have accumulated modest wealth. The legophobic individual is continuously and irrationally fearful of being sued. He protects himself with every kind of liability and catastrophe insurance available, but still retains an attorney on a full advice giving basis. He frequently calls his attorney late at night about matters where the possibility of legal consequences is extremely remote. He lives with the painful awareness of others who have "lost everything" in a law suit.

*"Go Ahead and Sue Me" Type:* The "go ahead and sue me" type is usually a judgment proof individual who masks his hostile and aggressive personality with legal verbiage. He has read a number of legal treatises and considers himself a legal expert. Anyone who challenges his business judgment, techniques or ethics is encouraged to try to interfere by suing him. He believes that when someone is reluctant or refuses to sue him, that it "proves" he was right all along.

*Legophilia:* The legophiliac seeks to correct all real and imagined wrongs done to him by suing. He tirelessly writes large corporations, local stores, doctors and dentists threatening to sue unless his demands for refunds or new goods and services are met. He seeks out one attorney after another, in a frenzied effort to find someone to take his case. When an attorney does consent to look into his claim but finds it without basis, the legophiliac threatens to sue the attorney for malpractice.

The legophiliac experiences an underlying paranoid reaction. Many times his cause is without foundation and irrational. He may explain to a district attorney that a neighbor is plotting to kill his cat or he may believe he has developed an invention which he asks a patent attorney to protect from foreign enemies. At other times, his cause may be valid, but his motivation is not to seek justice but vindication or punishment. In a recent case an attorney sought my advice about a legophiliac who was suing a company in a wrongful death suit on behalf of his son. The insurance company offered a $125,000.00 settlement which the plaintiff's lawyer thought was fair since the liability question was problematic. When he presented the offer to his client, the legophiliac became outraged, shouting that $125,000.00 was not enough "punishment." He also accused his lawyer of collaborating with the company from the outset.

How can an attorney communicate to the client that he's concerned about him as an individual, that he respects him, empathizes with his problem and intends to represent him in support of his rights and claims? When genuinely felt, the attorney can simply tell the client "I know how you must feel," "I'm angry about what has happened to you ' "I care about you and I'm concerned about your problem." A non-verbal method of expressing feelings toward a client is to vary physical interpersonal distance (PID). PID is the space an individual puts between himself and another while communicating.

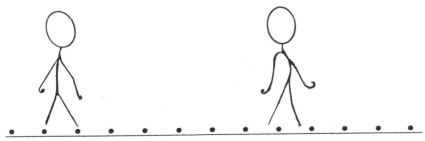

UNITS OF PHYSICAL INTERPERSONAL DISTANCE

Psychological studies indicate that attitudes and feelings for others can be measured through PID. Psychologist Bernard Addis at

58

the University of Oklahoma Medical School discovered that when two members of the opposite sex meet, males move closer to females, and females move closer to males than they would to their same sex. The phenomenon is predictably reversed for those who report being homosexual. These findings were obtained by tabulating the mean number of floor tiles between persons when they stop to meet each other in a university building. Dr. Addis also discovered that a reversal occurred when blacks and caucasians meet. White males approach closer to black males than to black females, and black females approach closer to white females than to white males.

Julius Fast in his book *Body Language* 23 explains that when a visitor is allowed to enter an executive's office or territory, the executive immediately gains superior status. How far the visitor goes in invading the territory suggests his own status. For example, does the visitor stop at the door, or walk across the room and shake hands? Structuring status in this way is not helpful to the attorney who wishes to put his client at ease and relate to him on a one to one basis wherein the client feels comfortable in revealing his true feelings. Fast also attaches significance to eye contact in relation to PID. In his chapter entitled "Winking, Blinking and Nods" he says that sneaking glances at a person reflects awkwardness. He reports on a study which indicates that during an interview, some interviewees avoided looking at the interviewer as much as 27% of the time. Awareness of the duration of client eye contact will sensitize the attorney to how comfortable the client is in the interview session which would reflect his strength as a potential witness.

PID is important in structuring the context in which the attorney interacts with the client as well as the manner in which he greets or leave him. Consider the typical law office design:

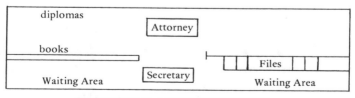

TRADITIONAL LAW OFFICE DESIGN

23. Julius Fast, BODY LANGUAGE, M. Evans and Co. Inc., 1970 pp. 37, 129.

The design suggests dignity and simplicity. Handsome furniture, diplomas, file cabinets, secretarial equipment and a reporter system are displayed. The design also suggests professionalism and efficiency. Colleagues easily identify with the decor, and it impresses them, but it does nothing for clients.

Women dress for other women, not for their spouses or boy friends. Similarly, attorneys design and furnish their offices for their colleagues and themselves, not for their clients. Analyzing the typical law office diagram, the client is projected as moving into the attorney's life space, but the attorney is not projected as penetrating the client's life space. The individual who never made an appointment with an attorney before, enters the law office as a stranger in a foreign and potentially hostile milieu. The waiting area is officiously removed from apparent activity; the secretary sits as a barrier to imposing wood-paneled doors. She may work at steel as opposed to wood furniture, suggesting reduced status. Once inside the attorney's inner office, the client is confronted with, and made uncomfortable by, a huge wood-grained desk on which is spread sharp objects such as pen sets and letter openers. However handsome, the scene represents threatening authority. The black framed diplomas and honors would elicit a sense of security in a more congenial context. Behind the desk looms the attorney in business grey or herringbone tweed. Luxurious carpeting can only make the client wonder what high fees must be charged. The client senses that there is no place for him in the general scheme of things.

No attorney consciously intends to intimidate his clients. And there is much he can do to assuage the client's anxiety, in order to make him feel a part of the process. As the client's discomfort increases, the effectiveness of the attorney's service diminishes. Why shouldn't the law office design contribute and complement legal service? Is it any wonder that clients lie to their attorneys in the prestige-polluted, law office environment. The surroundings themselves are an exaggeration. Consider the following client-centered office design, structured along social-psychological principles.

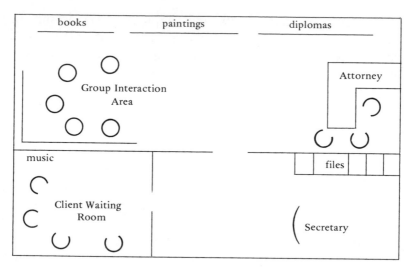

**CLIENT CENTERED LAW OFFICE DESIGN**

The optometrist asks his patients to sit in a dimly lit room for 10 minutes or so preceding an eye examination allowing the retina to dark-adapt to its surroundings. The law office waiting room should similarly allow the client an opportunity to adapt to the surroundings in which his interview and legal experience begin. One psychologist with a large metropolitan practice reportedly asks his patients to come for their appointments 20 minutes before schedule. This time is spent in a comfortable waiting room for purposes of relaxing from the tensions of the outside world. This psychologist has a gadget hooked up whereby the patient can signal the doctor of his arrival and though he is with another patient, the doctor signals the patient that he is in the office.

The client-centered office design retains the elements of professionalism and efficiency characteristic of the typical law office design. The difference lies in its life space orientation — it is client-centered. The client enters the suite to background music, blending into a relaxed contextual effect. A similar technique was experimented with some time ago by dentists who piped music to their patients through earphones. It was thought the music might be a substitute for novocaine and other desensitization drugs. Although the legal interview is seldom as physically painful as having a tooth pulled, from the client's point of view, it is often as anxiety provoking. That is why clients often "forget" their appointments.

The secretary or receptionist's desk in the client-centered office is oval and adjacent to, not in front of the client waiting area. If the secretary should assume an interested and extroverted attitude toward a new client, regardless of her estimates of his wealth, social status, ethnic background, and announces his arrival to the attorney via the intercom, her voice reflecting respect for the client, this complements the attorney's services. Unfortunately, many secretaries are respectful only to clients who they perceive as high status persons. The phenomenon exists in legal aid clinics only in reverse. There it is usually the low status person who gets the high status treatment. A secretary skilled at typing deeds, analyzing time sheets, and aiding in research, is not fulfilling her potential when she subtly reflects her own bias. Medium and larger sized law firms that can afford a receptionist with no other responsibilities than to greet clients, answer incoming calls and make appointments, should not leave hiring evaluation to an employment service.

Once I was asked to sit in on an interview conducted by an attorney looking for a new receptionist. The attorney introduced himself and began explaining to the applicant the kind of law he practiced, the names and interests of his partners. He also told her where he went to school and shared a comical law school experience. When the interview was over, he told me he was impressed by the applicant. I, too, was impressed by her ability to listen, but knew precious little else about her motivation, education, skills and interest. The secretary who answers the phone and greets clients has as much control over the success of the law practice as the senior partner.

After greeting the client, the attorney should instruct his secretary to hold all calls. This dramatizes the client's importance. So do the furnishings of the inner areas of the office which are comfortable. The attorney assumes a relaxed body position and the desk becomes merely something to write on and not a blockade. Auto-mated typewriters, the MTST, XEROX, microfilm readers and dicta-phones become tools to increase service efficiency and not weapons.

Depending on anticipated interview time and the nature of the advice given, the attorney should invite the client to the group inter-action area where seats are equal in comfort and allow the legal counselor and his client to attack a problem on a physically equal basis. Warm colors and abstract paintings tend to relax the client, allowing him to project himself into his surroundings. Diplomas and honors which may include license to practice, law degree, and a pro-fessional society are useful. But a wall studded with certificates such as 1,000,000 mile airline clubs, appointments to admiralty by politicians for a day, and photographs of skiing at Vail only tend to confuse. Confidence is evoked by an ample supply of law reference materials even though a more complete library is maintained else-where. On occasion, the attorney may want to create an uncomfort-able atmosphere when he takes a deposition or is driving a hard bar-gain with an adversary. In this event, more authority, more structure and less flexibility are indicated.

Why go to all this trouble in office and furnishing. First, because it isn't more trouble, and second, it is no more expensive than the typical office design. Third, it is client-centered, adapting the client to legal services, lowering the threshold of his defense mechanisms and increasing the probability of honest and productive appointment sessions. By utilizing psychological interactional principles, the client-centered approach eliminates or lessens the undesirable pro-pensity to overestimate a positive legal outcome as in, "There's no doubt in my mind we can win this case," or "this case will easily bring a $50,000 judgment."

The first 30 to 60 minutes the attorney spends with his client are critical. In psychotherapy, it can take as many as 2-6 visits to establish psychologist-patient rapport and guidelines for the dynamic interaction to follow. The attorney's problem is vastly more complex since he must establish rapport as well as achieve his primary goal of legal interviewing at the same time. When the attorney considers and responds to the client's needs, the client develops a more positive view toward the attorney's competency and resourcefulness, and a more optimistic view of the legal process. Fifteen years ago, industrial psychologists jolted the business community by publishing research findings which indicated employees were more concerned with job satisfaction, security, and congenial surroundings than with hourly wages. Later studies produced similar findings for corporate executives. Economists tell us our society is essentially capitalist but this does not necessarily mean every human motive is satiated by financial remuneration. For his part, the client is more concerned with his identity, his sense of fair play, and of being treated with respect than with winning his case. This principle is understood by the effective legal counselor and overlooked or repressed by the legal mechanic who views the problem, not the client, the remedy, not the reaction to it, as controlling. The generic relationship between attorney and client has much in common with the physician-patient, priest-parishioner, shaman-tribal member and father-son relationships. The legal term "fiduciary" hints at the potentially deep and meaningful, interpersonal nature of attorney-client rapport.

## THE ATTORNEY AS THERAPIST

Our chapter began with a young attorney's reflection: "From my divorce cases, I realize some clients are willing to stay all day to discuss their social problems if I permit it." The hospitalized client calls the attorney complaining about an automobile accident which the attorney characteristically perceives as a legal problem; but for the client, it is a medical and psychological problem with legal aspects. Similarly, a patient may have committed a crime, which for the psychologist is a personality problem, but for the patient it is a legal problem with psychological implications. Although the legal aspect is beyond the psychologist's competency to deal with, he does not cut off the patient by saying, "I'm sorry, you've just described a legal problem, let's try to direct our conversation to your emotional reaction to it." The psychologist listens, probes and explores even though 30 minutes of the patient's appointment is absorbed in the process. He is concerned with the whole individual which includes legal involvements. At this juncture, the psychologist and the attorney are complementary, each trained to relate to a different dimension of the same behavior. The attorney, though on a contingent fee, may charge for consultation time. With this approach, it is not financially burdening to listen to the client describe his emotions. A client's feelings are involved in all the legal issues he is confronted with, and are especially strong in criminal cases, in estate planning, in divorce, in labor negotiations and in forming a corporation or partnership. Dr. Michael Nash, a forensic psychologist, observed:

> It is necessary for the attorney to pay attention to what he may consider irrelevancies which the client is telling him. The attorney must also be careful that in his abstraction of the legal reality from the client's description, to bridge the client's view of the situation to the legal situation keeping in mind at all times that the bridge must be satisfactory to the client's framework of fairness. In order to do this, the attorney must be aware of the therapeutic aspect of his personality.

The successful attorney concentrates on legal problems and is highly skilled to help in that way, but he realizes that he must relate legal solutions to personal drives, motives and fears. A legal problem may be most effectively disposed of by legal counseling and not through filing a suit. A psychologist may conclude that an individual's marriage is more damaging than rewarding and help the individual explore the potential value of a legal remedy to his psychological trauma, i.e. divorce. The fallacy of categorizing or diagnosing a problem as exclusively legal or psychological is illustrated by the holding in Laube vs. Stevenson,[24] a Connecticut case.

> Plaintiff brought the action against her daughter and son-in-law to recover for personal injuries sustained by a fall on a cellar stairway in the defendants' home due to negligence. The stairway led from the kitchen to the cellar and was in a defective and dangerous condition. No light fixture was present. The defendants had prior knowledge of the condition which was further

---

24. LAUBE vs. STEVENSON, 137 Conn. 469

exacerbated by a vacuum cleaner placed to one side of the landing.

Injury occurred when the defendant's daughter asked the plaintiff to go to the cellar and bring a blanket for her baby, but failed to warn her about the dangerous landing condition. Descending the stairs, plaintiff slipped and fell violently to the cellar floor.

The court held that plaintiff was a gratuitous licensee, not a business visitor and that although the defendant daughter had an affirmative duty to warn, the defendant's husband was free from liability because he had no knowledge that plaintiff would use the satirs or that his wife would be his agent in making the request. The dissent raised the question of why a social visitor should not receive the same protection accorded an invitee.

The court's discussion of liability of an invitee vis a vis to a licensee, was erudite, yet ignored the social reality underlying the case: a mother sued her daughter and son-in-law over injuries received while retrieving her grandchild's blanket. Attorney for the plaintiff was not dealing with an indigenous legal problem, but with a clinical problem involving legal complications. It was not clear whether this was a friendly suit or whether daughter and son-in-law were insured.

## TIME

The relationship between attorney and client is bounded in the fourth dimension (time) as in all legal procedure. The practicing attorney must record chargable time. There is a specific time to file suit, to go to trial, render verdicts, to appeal, etc. A suit not filed within a certain prescribed time is barred by the statute of limitatation. A plaintiff who waits too long before taking legal action may be barred by the equitable doctrine of laches. The effective attorney is sensitized to his client's perception and expectations of time and attempts to keep the client informed as to the progress of professional services in time units. The more accurate the prediction of time requirements, the more useful it is for the client. Overly enthusiastic predictions only create disappointment in the attorney's ability to effect results. The widow who understands the length of probate and the client who understands the time-residency requirements for divorce are better set psychologically for the legal process and more appreciative of the attorney's position. The impatient franchisee who is advised that a complete evaluation of the franchise opportunity will involve several months to consider sales data, credit terms, rent and equipment, etc., is disappointed initially, but grateful later. Perhaps no other factor is as important in effectuating out of court settlements than the fear of long, drawnout court battles.

In negotiating settlements, Royce A. Coffin, author of *The Negotiator*, [25] provides simple, but prudent advice — "sleep on it—do not yield to pressure for an immediate decision which is usually unnecessary anyway." He also warns against marathon sessions since tired negotiators don't perform well and staying power won't impress the other side. Coffin suggests that when the mission is accomplished the negotiator should leave. Some lawyers apparently have the self defeating personality characteristic of continuing to talk endlessly until they say the wrong thing.

Terminating the legal interview should be definite although warm and personal. Some patients tend to feel the therapist doesn't like them or is only interested in his fee when he refuses to linger past the 45 or 50 minute appointment. But gradually, hostility diminishes and trust develops as the patient realizes that termination only means that allotted time has passed. Continuous glancing at the therapist's watch, as a not so subtle technique, then becomes unnecessary.

Parents expend considerable energy in teaching their children to tell time, and usually mark success with some ado, like presenting the child with his first watch. Today's watches count the hour, second, month and day and stress the accuracy perhaps to a greater extent than will be necessary for human scheduling over the next 10 to

25. Royce Coffin, THE NEGOTIATOR, 1973, Amalon, New York.

15 years. Modern understanding of time can be traced to Einstein's notion of time bending in space and the computer's capacity to slice a second a thousand ways.

In the not too distant future we will have to learn other systems of time than earth time. It will be necessary for us to read lunar and solar time. The first moon watch was developed by Elgin National Industries based on the moon's light-dark cycle for 29.53 earth days. But speaking of a "day" on the moon will be confusing. The astronomical term for a moon cycle is "lunation." Each lunation is broken down into 30 lunes, each about the length of one earth day. Each lune is divided into 20 lunours, approximately as long as each hour on earth.

Modern life is time-oriented and schedule-oriented, although important cultural and subcultural differences exist. Emphasis on time varies dramatically from New York to the Vietnamese hamlet. Establishing a hot line between Washington and Moscow reflects the belief by diplomats that the survival of the human race is inextricably bound by time measurement. American soldiers stationed at the North and South Pole report confusion and irritation at extreme variations in the length of sun light and darkness. Sensory deprivation studies, where individuals are confined to floating in water tanks without cues to times or any other stimulation such as sounds, sight, taste, etc., indicate that psychotic symptoms of disorientation, hallucinations and loss of contact with reality develop under these conditions. Subjects frequently believe a day has passed in a period of 2 to 3 hours. Biological data suggests that the human organism itself is time oriented which allows man to decide to sleep for three and one-half hours, and without the aid of an alarm clock, wake up precisely at the end of that duration.

Quinine and alcohol create the illusion that time passes slowly while mescaline and marijuana have a more inconsistent effect, causing errors in time judgment as well as pathological reactions. A propensity has been observed to regard time as a possession. Consider expressions such as "all I have is time," or "and this too shall pass." Psychologist John Cohen at the University of Manchester made an important analysis of man's relationship to time. Dr. Cohen[26] observes that time is regarded as a personal possession that one can give, waste or save. He notes that when the Gregorian calendar was adopted in England and September 3, 1752 became September 14, riots broke out as the populace believed they had "lost" 11 days from their lives.

An individual's perception of time is a function of his personality, physiology and the situational context in which he finds himself. One attorney who was a patient of mine became emotionally disturbed for a period of time as a result of family crises. During this period he allowed the statute of limitation to lapse for an important personal injury case he was handling for a client. Although the Court admonished him for "forgetfulness," we know that during periods of stress, time is distorted. For mentally healthy individuals, time is also an individual experience. The reader may wish to probe his or her concept of time by marking off on the line below the following life experiences: (1) first date (2) graduation from college (3) point of greatest personal achievement (4) the present.

_____

Birth                                                      Death

## ATTORNEY-CLIENT INTIMACY

The attorney typically greets male clients with a handshake. Over the past several years, it has become customary to greet female clients in the same way. Since the handshake is the first and generally only physical interaction between the attorney and his client, it becomes significant. Psychologists Secord and Backman[27] have observed:

> A flabby handshake may suggest lack of warmth; jerky, erratic movements may indicate nervousness; sweeping, expansive gestures may suggest force and vigor; and constraint of movement with accompanying stiffness of manner may imply aloofness and reserve.

26. J. Cohen, "PSYCHOLOGICAL TIME", Scientific American, Nov. 1964, p. 2.
27. Secord and Backman, Social Psychology, 1964.

Recent trends in psychotherapy have encouraged doctor-patient touching as a means of expressing empathy and warmth. Writing for the *Duke Law Review,* lawyer Donald Davidoff[28] concludes that current case law does not preclude the therapist from putting his arm around a patient who is crying, or distraught. The session in which the lawyer counsels his client about divorce may be as emotionally laden as when the patient discusses the same material with the psychologist.

Dr. Clifford Knape, Texas Veterans' Hospital Chief of Psychological Service, recently demonstrated the therapeutic aspects of human touch in a group psycho-drama. A schizophrenic Vietnam veteran with paranoic beliefs was encouraged to act out critical life experiences. Hospital staff members played the role of his parents, siblings, army sergeant and high school principal. Knape, white-haired and epitomizing the father figure image, sensed the young man's isolation and feelings of distrust. At the end of the drama, Knape approached him and put his arm around his shoulder describing and explaining the drama's implications and sharing his observations. As the group looked on, he summoned a matronly looking nurse who hugged the patient. As a result, the patient responded with more spontaneous speech and intelligent insights about his experience. He appeared visably moved by the group's affection.

It is not suggested that attorneys become affectionate with their clients. However, handshaking, postural stance and reassuring or supportive gestures provide overt means of demonstrating concern and empathy in the process of legal problem solving.

Voice communication is a critical, but often neglected aspect of legal practice. The attorney communicates through voice by telephone, in his office and in the courtroom. Research indicates that individuals are able to reach consensus as to whether a voice is warm, cold or neutral. Sound waves are physical when received and transmitted to the temporal area of the cortex. But they are interpreted by the brain psychologically. Dr. Morton Cooper, audiologist

---

28. 1966 Duke Law Review 696, "MALPRACTICE OF PSYCHIATRISTS."

at the UCLA Medical Center, in an article entitled "Vocal Suicide in the Legal Profession," described the need for voice awareness of study, especially as regards what he has labeled, "the attorney's confidential voice."

> Imagine yourself physically close to someone; your tendency is to lower the volume of your voice, and to drop its pitch. The quality of voice may change from a sharp, well-placed tone to a throaty tone, guttural or gruff, or to a very mellow tone.

> The lower register can produce such a timbre, but this confidential voice is different from the normal speaking voice. It is the voice of the person who is saying, "This is something I wish you to keep to yourself." A lawyer often uses the confidential voice for a knowing, reassuring approach.

> Using the confidential voice too often or too persistently, the lawyer confronts a clear and present danger that his voice will not be usable for very long. In time, vocal fatigue will almost always develop.[29]

## ETHNICITY

The effective attorney avoids stereotyping clients along ethnic dimensions and also avoids assigning stereotypic ethnic characteristics to such individuals. Psychologist Gregory Razran illustrated the fallacy of stereotypes by showing 30 ethnically non-specific photos of females' faces to a group of college students. Ethnically non-specific means that a prior group of students could not agree on the ethnic background of the faces.

The students were asked to rate each photograph indicating the degree of liking the face, its beauty, intelligence, character, ambition and entertainingness. Two months later, the same students were again shown the photos but with Italian, Irish, Jewish and other ethnic surnames added beneath the photographs. Thus a previously unidentified photo now had a name added under it such as Sally O'Hare,

---

29. M. Cooper, 75 Case and Comment 42, "VOCAL SUICIDE IN THE LEGAL PROFESSION."

Shelia Capponella or Roberta Finklestein. By labeling in this way, the investigator was able to show that categorizing the photos ethnically had a striking effect on the way in which the photographs were perceived.

Psychologist E. L. Hartley further dramatized the fallacy of stereotyping by presenting research subjects with a list of 35 ethnic groups and asking them to assign favorable and unfavorable personality traits to the groups. Within the list, Hartley planted three fictitious groups: the Danerians, the Perienians and the Wallonians. The subjects showed no hesitation in rating these non-existent groups. Not surprisingly, they assigned to them a high percentage of unfavorable traits. The attorney's task is to communicate his interest and concern for the client. This becomes especially critical when the white attorney represents the black client or the black attorney represents the white client.

## THE INTERVIEW

Good interview techniques are vital to a client's feelings of adequacy, security and to his assessment of the attorney's resourcefulness and competency. Effective interviewing techniques also emphasize to the client that the attorney is on his side. The "you have a problem and I am on your side" transaction is as difficult for the attorney to cope with as for the psychotherapist. Psychiatrist Robert Lindner notes that the patient comes to protest his reaction to society's rules and is led to adjust to the rules instead of being encouraged to change them, or rebel against them. The criminal attorney like the doctor, may lose the confidence of his client if he is seen as society's agent. As Lindner observes:[30]

> We are, therefore, I believe, entitled to say that most of the accomplishments proudly claimed by members of these professional groups—most of the magic advertised by psychiatry, some of what passes for psychoanalysis, much of clinical psychology, all of religion, and a good deal of the less pretentious arts of medicine and social service—is based upon a cult of

30. Robert Lindner, PRESCRIPTION FOR REBELLION, Grove Press, Inc., New York; 1952, pp. 16-17.

passivity and surrender. The transformations worked by the application of these disciplines are founded upon renunciation and little more. Such wonder-working claims as they make are, thus, by and large specious; and to speak of their "successes" as "cures," or as profound alterations of lasting individual or social benefit, is to pile falsehood upon untruth. They operate chiefly by the process of weaning a sufferer from the form of protest which expressed his woe, and they broadly ignore the woe itself.

Suppose a client makes an appointment to see an attorney, describes an automobile accident in which he was injured, and asks the counselor's advice. In the typical personal injury interview, the following questions are likely to be asked:

1. Where did the accident occur?
2. At what time?
3. Who was driving the other car?
4. Was anyone else in the other car?
5. Who was driving your car?
6. Were there any passengers in your car?
7. Were there any witnesses to the accident?
8. How did the accident happen?
9. Was anything said directly after the accident?
10. Who called the police?
11. Was a ticket issued?
12. Are you insured?
13. What injuries did you sustain?
14. What doctor did you visit?
15. What medication and treatment was administered?
16. Do you still have symptoms of the injury?
17. What was the condition of the various cars after the accident?
18. What was the condition of your car before the accident?

Such questions are central to the development of pleadings, proof, instructions and remedies, but other more projective questions are required for zeroing in on the client's needs and expectations:

1. What do you think will happen in this situation?
2. What would you like to see happen?
3. Do you understand the time involved in resolving your problem?

Questions 1—3 allow the client to tell about his feelings, attitudes and desires. By listening carefully, and by probing his responses, the attorney begins to develop a more meaningful relationship with his client.

Throughout the interview process, effective attorneys are sensitive to cues of client discomfort. Such cues are treated at length in Chapter 6. Sweating, trembling and twitching reflect the significance of certain questions. Psychological research indicates that when the client is responding positively to questions or answers, there will be increased eye contact between himself and the interviewer, whereas eye contact decreases significantly when the interviewee is experiencing negative effect. Negative emotional effect is revealed in pupil contraction and is suggested by folded arms and crossed legs, which are symbolic barriers to physical interaction or protection from attack.

Involving a client in the preparation of his own case is rewarding to both attorney and client. Clients frequently have excellent insights into methods of proof which can be elicited during a group problem solving or "brain storming" session. During "brain storming," the attorney invites his client and one or two associates to join him for a conference. An idea or theory of recovery is presented and all participants must try to improve on the theory, exploring its ramifications and discussing what forms of evidence it might involve. No one is allowed to criticize the theory or idea under consideration and each participant must attempt to improve it while relating it to the facts of the case.

The opposing side's case must also be brain stormed. If you were they, what assertions and defenses would you urge? This must be done with objectivity and detachment. So often attorneys don't view their opponent's strengths realistically. A participating client will develop a sense of involvement in the preparation of his case, will become appreciative of the complex nature of the attorney's services, and will also begin to feel responsibility for its outcome. Brain storming can produce creative approaches and valuable insights.

The principles and perspectives provided in this chapter are directed toward enhancing the quality of the attorney – client rapport. The client wants to view himself at the center of the legal process for his case. If the attorney encourages this feeling, he will increase the likelihood that the client will perceive the attorney as "his attorney" or "the family lawyer" or "our corporation attorney." In addition to charging the client a specific sum for writing a will, filing a divorce, appealing a case, etc., the attorney should charge an hourly rate for consultation. In this way, adopting the client – centered approach will not be a financial burden. Utilizing this approach, the attorney may lose a case, but seldom a client.

# chapter 4

# Jury Selection

Three psychologists helped pick the jury for the trial of Angela Davis in one of the most highly publicized proceedings of the 1970's. They set out to accomplish what seemed to defense counsels an almost impossible mission—to choose an impartial jury to sit in judgment of a black militant woman who was an avowed communist. She was acquitted.[31] In 1972, forensic psychologist Jay Shulman, worked beside defense attorney and former U.S. Attorney General Ramsey Clark in the selection of jurors for the conspiracy trial of the Harrisburg Seven which included Father Philip Berrigan and Sister Elizabeth McAlister. The jury hung 10 - 2 in favor of acquittal.[32] Physician-Psychologist, William Bryant, Jr. aided attorney F. Lee Bailey in selecting the jury for the trial of Dr. Sam Sheppard, the neurosurgeon accused of murdering his wife. The defense maintained that Mrs. Sheppard was killed by a bushy-haired man who had also struck Dr. Sheppard unconscious. Sheppard's innocence was established to the jury's satisfaction. A television series, *The Fugitive*, starring David Janssen was based in part on Dr. Sheppard's life.

In Dallas and Houston, Texas, psychologist Michael Gottlieb and I consulted in the selection of juries for personal injury cases where lawyers were concerned that they would not be able to identify and strike potentially biased or prejudiced jurors. The results were the highest jury awards for their clients in the legal history of the two cities. In the Houston cases, attorneys John O'Quinn and Will Watkins represented the plaintiffs and the jury awards were $680,000 and $1,700,000 respectively. In the Dallas case, Windle Turley, attorney for the plaintiff and an expert on the crashworthiness of airplanes, recovered $400,000 for his client. We also consulted in the selection of a jury for the Cundiff murder trial in Dallas. Defended by criminal defense specialist, Charles Tessmer, Mrs. Cundiff was acquitted of murder despite the testimony of a discredited eyewitness who reportedly saw the defendant leaving the deceased's house carrying the murder weapon.

Psychological methodology applied to the study of the jury process has historically been viewed with suspicion. The legal pro-

---

31. W. Sage, "Psychology and the Angela Davis Jury," HUMAN BEHAVIOR," 1973 Vol. 2, pp. 56-61.
32. J. Schulman, et al: "Recipe for a Jury," PSYCHOLOGY TODAY, May 1973, p. 37.

fession has been reticent to place the important function of jury selection in the hands of non-lawyers, fearing that one not trained in law could not have the perspective required to intelligently select a jury. Another objection is fairness. While lecturing to the Southern California District Attorney's Association, prosecutors expressed to me their frustration because it is more difficult for the state to budget the consultation of a psychologist than for defense lawyers. The third objection is constitutional—that the consultation of psychologists in jury selection may violate due process and constitute an invasion of privacy.

In 1954 under a $400,000 grant from the Ford Foundation to study the judicial process, a prominent group of University of Chicago jurists and behavioral scientists "bugged" a juryroom in order to record and analyze jury deliberations along psychological dimensions. On October 12, 1955, a congressional subcommittee of the Senate Judiciary Committee under the Internal Security Act[33] held hearings to investigate both the jury "bugging" incident and a subsequent presentation of its recorded product at the 10th Judicial Conference at Estes Park, Colorado. The Conference was an august body of distinguished attorneys and judges and was attended by Supreme Court Justice Tom Clark.

Congressional inquiry fixated on the possibility of communist subversion. The Dean and Project Director of the Chicago Law School was quizzed about a letter he had written years earlier critical of the House Un-American Activities Committee. It was also established that the Dean knew a Chicago student who considered himself to be a communist and that the Dean had contributed to the American Civil Liberties Union. The Dean was misguided, but no communist. In 1975 President Ford appointed him to become the United States District Attorney.

The scientists and lawyers involved in the project expressed devotion for and faith in the jury process, but the jury bugging incident admittedly was wrong. It invaded the privacy of 12 individuals without their permission. For this reason, the jury process is currently studied by using mock juries and staged trials. What is lost in realism is gained in the protection of basic freedoms, and in science, approximation of actual conditions is always legitimate. The NASA

33. Committee on Judiciary, "Recording of Jury Deliberations," 1955 pursuant to S. Res. 58.

78

Space team, for example, didn't have to send a man to the moon in order to develop the technology to send a man to the moon. The weakness of mock jury studies, like all laboratory studies of human behavior, is that they can lead to invalid conclusions if their artificiality is not taken into account. Generalizations from such studies must be made with caution.

The American Bar Association Code of Professional responsibility maintains appropriately high standards for the protection of veniremen* and jurors.

> EC 7-29 To safeguard the impartiality that is essential to the judicial process, veniremen and jurors should be protected against extraneous influences. When impartiality is present, public confidence in the judicial system is enhanced. There should be no extrajudicial communication with veniremen prior to trial or with jurors during trial by or on behalf of a lawyer connected with the case. Furthermore, a lawyer who is not connected with the case should not communicate with or cause another to communicate with a venireman or a juror about the case. After the trial, communication by a lawyer with jurors is permitted so long as he refrains from asking questions or making comments that tend to harass or embarrass the juror or to influence actions of the juror in future cases. Were a lawyer to be prohibited from communicating after trial with a juror, he could not ascertain if the verdict might be subject to legal challenge, in which event the invalidity of a verdict might go undetected. When an extrajudicial communication by a lawyer with a juror is permitted by law, it should be made considerately and with deference to the personal feelings of the juror.

> EC 7-30 Vexatious or harassing investigations of veniremen or jurors seriously impair the effectiveness of our jury system. For this reason, a lawyer or anyone on his behalf who conducts an investigation of veniremen or jurors should act with circumspection and restraint.

*For non-lawyers, a venireman is a person called for jury service to the courthouse. He becomes part of the panel from which the jury is selected.

EC 7-31 Communications with or investigations of members of families of veniremen or jurors by a lawyer or by anyone on his behalf are subject to the restrictions imposed upon the lawyer with respect to his communications with or investigations of veniremen and jurors.

EC 7-32 Because of his duty to aid in preserving the integrity of the jury system, a lawyer who learns of improper conduct by or towards a venireman, a juror, or member of the family of either should make a prompt report to the court regarding such conduct.

From an ethical point of view, the role of the psychologist must be to aid in the selection of a fair and unbiased jury, a jury that will not be predisposed, prior to hearing evidence, to be antagonistic to the lawyer, the client or to the cause of action.

In state courts, veniremen are called to service by a variety of methods of which the most common is selection from tax rolls and voter registration lists. Other criteria of selection are: age, citizenship, literacy, health, mental capacity and the lack of a criminal record. Qualifications for federal jurors are prescribed by the United States Code and Federal Rule of Civil Procedure 38. Names of prospective jurors are typically placed in a rotating device or jury wheel, which hypothetically insures randomness within the wheel. Because of the methods of selecting names, the names themselves are not representative of residents or inhabitants within the jurisdiction. Exemptions and excuses which permit a citizen to avoid jury service when called increase the likelihood of a biased selection and may violate the equal protection clause of the 14th Amendment.

## THOSE COMMONLY EXEMPTED FROM JURY SERVICE

1. Judges of any court of record, justices of the peace
2. Sheriffs, deputies, constables, jailers and persons having custody of State or Federal prisoners

3. Licensed attorneys engaged in the practice of law
4. Habitual drunkards
5. Persons afflicted with a bodily infirmity amounting to a disability
6. Anyone convicted of an infamous crime or serving a term in a penetentiary for committing a felony

## THOSE COMMONLY EXCUSED
## FROM JURY SERVICE

1. Persons over 65 years of age
2. Ministers of the gospel
3. County and district officials
4. Practicing physicians, optometrists, veterinarians, dentists, undertakers, pharmacists, teachers in the public school
5. Postmasters and U. S. mail carriers
6. Members of the National Guard
7. Persons engaged or employed in the publication of a newspaper
8. Members of a regularly organized fire department
9. All women with minor children

The list of exemptions and excuses demonstrates that American juries are ultimately composed of individuals not excluded, rather than those selected. Professional persons can nearly always be excused and frequently request to be excused. Except in the case of blue ribbon or special juries, a jury composed of middle class home-owners and lower class voters is inevitable. A Los Angeles survey revealed jury rooms packed with housewives, clerical workers, craftsmen, and retired persons. In a Chicago study, a marked increase in the number of female jurors was observed in addition to a statistical regression toward average educational achievement.

## MYTHS AND FACTS

The emergence of the middle class jury phenomenon creates difficulties for the attorney on voir dire, especially as regards his allotment of pre-emptory challenges. Challenges for cause are more obvious: an interested party, a relative, friend of close business associate of the opposing party.* Socio-economic differences among prospective jurors precipitate differential attitudes toward crimes, and the facts and law of civil disputes. Middle class individuals are more threatened by crimes against property and violent crimes than by white collar crimes such as embezzlement, tax evasion and forgery. The middle class in America represents the consumer class and the future of the free enterprise system is in a large measure moored to their welfare. Current abuses in consumer practices by some businesses have led to the Truth in Lending Act, development of the implied warranties, the presidential appointment of an advisor on consumer affairs, and the respect shown for Harvard educated attorney, Mr. Ralph Nader. In the Muckraker tradition of Lincoln Steffens, he and his staff have scrutinized the marketing of products from toys to tractors. It was not until irresponsible business interests attempted to depreciate his efforts by labeling him a homosexual that his real popularity surged. Middle class individuals, particularly the housewife and the inflation poor non-managerial white collar worker make excellent jurors for the plaintiff in products liability cases and suits against corporations. Typically only management level personnel with high aspiration levels can identify with the corporation, a legal entity devoid of human characteristics.

In selecting the jury, a physiognomic approach has apparently enjoyed popularity among some attorneys, though professor of law, S. W. McCart in his text, *Trial by Jury*, provides an example of the fallacy:[34]

> The meeting of the eyebrows and closely knit eyes indicate narrow mindedness, having an upper eyelid cover more than a third of the iris suggests secretiveness, the short upper lip is responsive to harm.

This approach is easily invalidated by behavioral science research. It assumes a like status with astrology and palm reading as quasi-

---

* (Note for non-lawyers) In Texas, each side is entitled to an unlimited number of challenges for cause. In criminal cases, each side receives ten pre-emptory strikes and six strikes in civil cases. Adjustments are made in the case of multiple defendants or plaintiffs.
34. S. McCart, TRIAL BY JURY, copyright 1965 by S. McCart. Reprinted by permission of Chilton Book Company, Philadelphia, p. 35.

science or non-science. On January 17, 1969, it was announced by Merck-Sharp Dohme Research Laboratories and Rockefeller University that the enzyme ribonuclease which plays a key role in hereditary determinants was synthesized in a laboratory. Some months later, Jack Griffith, a graduate student at the California Institute of Technology, succeeded in photographing the DNA molecule, which controls hereditary characteristics. When biochemists are able to crack the genetic code and artificially synthesize life itself, and actually restructure gene linkages, the physiognomic approach should be re-evaluated.

Physical features and constitutional factors are relevant cues to a venireman's predisposition to respond. Some lawyers have written that balding men are more likely to be responsive to a female plaintiff claiming loss of hair due to chemical "treatments" applied at the local beauty parlor and that athletically oriented men are likely to be more sympathetic to a plaintiff who has lost a limb than those who are more introverted. Some lawyers have observed that less endowed women are likely to be hostile toward a buxom female. One curious study indicated that ectomorphs (thin persons) provide lower damage awards in civil cases than do mesomorphs (athletic), or endomorphs (heavy persons). Sheldon's somatology, discussed in Chapter I, illustrated the effect of constitutional factors on self concept, but inferences to personality traits from constitutional variations should be made with great caution.

Nierenberg and Calero,[35] in their treatise on body language *How to Read a Person Like a Book,* have made a useful beginning classification for gestures and postures which have significance in American culture. Some of their concepts are summarized below:

| GESTURE/POSTURE | SIGNIFICANCE |
| --- | --- |
| Open hands | Sincerity, openness |
| Unbuttoning coat | Agreement is possible |
| Arms crossed on chest | Defensiveness |
| Arm or leg over chair | Indifference |

35.  G. Nierenberg and H. Calero, HOW TO READ A PERSON LIKE A BOOK, Cornerstone Library, New York, 1971.

| | |
|---|---|
| Female crossing legs with slight kicking motion | Boredom |
| Hand to cheek or chin stroking | Evaluation gesture |
| Eyeglasses dropping over nose bridge | Negative reaction |
| Nose rubbing | Negative reaction |
| Joining fingertips | Confidence, egotism |
| Leaning back with hands laced behind head | Relaxed aggressiveness |
| Throat clearing | Nervousness |

Ethnicity as a variable should be weighed in predicting juror attitudes where cultural or subcultural values are believed to have a direct impact. Studies indicate that jurors of German and British descent tend to favor the state's position in criminal proceedings, whereas Blacks, Italians, and persons of Slavic descent tend to vote for the defendant. This outcome may be accounted for by identification and introjection—modern societies in Great Britain and Germany have emphasized respect for law and as in the traditional Japanese family, have succeeded in transmitting this respect to youth. Until recently, for example, British police officers or bobbies, did not carry guns when patrolling their beats. Blacks, Italians, and persons of Slavic descent represent minority groups within American culture and thereby become more sensitized to abuses of majority created and enforced law. Attorney Louis Katz,[36] writing for the magazine *Trial,* cites lawyers who believe that Latins are emotional and Orientals conservative, and Jews, liberal, and Central Europeans, conservative. Such generalizations are dangerous since there are usually as many attitude differences within an ethnic group as between ethnic groups. Keith Mossman, Chairman of the American Bar Association Criminal Law Section, having reviewed the ethnic generalities has lamented that in all of his years as a practicing lawyer in Iowa, he has yet to encounter what must be the ideal juror—a Spanish carpenter.

In western civilization, emphasis, respect and social deference were traditionally directed toward increased age. "Respect your

36. L. Katz, "The Twelve Man Jury," TRIAL, December, 1969, p. 39.

elders;" "Give your seat to that lady;" "You'll understand that when you're older." All were once familiar admonitions to children and adolescents. Today, youth appears dissatisfied with such arrangements: youth are better educated, more informed and generally better traveled than their parents. They view their youthfulness as an asset and not as a liability, and adults, as reflected in movies, cosmetic ads and poetry, now make a fetish of youthfulness. Young people today tend to sense their favored stage of maturation and development. Because of the identification process, a younger jury will provide more tolerance and insight where a defendant or litigant is young and his position is directed wholly or in part against adult type rules, i.e. drug abuse, draft evasion and delinquent behavior. Youth are more likely to understand an insanity defense and be concerned with rehabilitation, but peer group jurors are more likely to sense dishonesty and the camouflaging of motives which leads to a boomerang effect. College students consistently give poorer grades to their classmates in experimental grading classes than would an instructor; experimental traffic court juries composed of teenagers are notoriously more punitive than actual judges for peer group offenders.

Books about trial preparation stress preparation of the client or witness through coaching which includes appropriate attitude and dress. Emphasis is on anticipation since many trial attorneys think it risky to examine a witness when the response is not fully expected. Some have suggested that the female client or witness be dressed in a sexually provocative way in order to curry the favor of male jurors. This advice is ludicrous. At the unconscious level males often experience a need to punish a woman overtly flirtatious and even subtly seductive. Moreover, female jurors may be threatened or feel hostile. Professor Broeder at the University of Chicago cites the case of an attractive 22-year-old mother in a wrongful death action. Her counsel argued damages based on her deceased husband's life expectancy and potential earning power. In awarding only one-half of the requested damages, the jury reasoned that a woman as attractive as the plaintiff certainly would marry within a year or two and that her failure to do so would not be the defendant's responsibility. Coaching or preparation of a witness in isolation of analysis of who is to receive the information, is wasted energy.

The concepts of jury selections discussed to this point are generalizations and as Oliver Wendell Holmes observed "No generalization is worth a damn." Age, sex, religion, marital status may be relevant factors for a particular case but not in every case. A Dallas prosecutor who represented the State in the Jack Ruby Trial pushed the generalization concept so far as to be critical of jurors whose occupations begin with the letter "p." This would include "pimps, preachers, psychologists, professors, physicians and pipe smokers." In his book, *The Chosen Ones,*[37] Dr. Bryan suggests that his hypnotic suggestive techniques "enable us to look into the mind of the prospective juror, discover his prejudices and predict which way he will vote on a given set of facts and circumstances." This statement is fascinating but also general and grandiose. Nor will observing body language alone yield a fair and impartial jury. Nor will the development of attitude questionnaires to test authoritarianism do the job, as suggested by a *Kentucky Law Journal* article.[38] Nothing short of a comprehensive empirical analysis of numerous psychological and sociological factors and an assessment of their relative importance will be of any use in jury selection.

## A NEW TECHNIQUE

Step 1. Counsel apprises client of his intention to consult with a forensic psychologist on the matter of jury selection and solicits his client's approval. Where the client participates in decision-making, he holds counsel and the legal process in higher esteem.

Step 2. Attorney provides psychologist with a fact situation summary which includes legal issues and a description of critical witnesses and what they are anticipated to testify about. In other words, the psychologist must have at least a general grasp of the case (approximately 30 minutes dictation).

Step 3. Psychologist informally evaluates counsel over matters rele-

---

37. W. Bryan, Jr., THE CHOSEN ONES, Vantage Press, New York, 1971, pp. 23, 74.
38. D. Emerson, "Personality Tests for Prospective Jurors," KENTUCKY LAW JOURNAL, 1968, Volume 56, pp. 832-854.

vant to court room style. This includes observation of dress, speech patterns and personality dynamics. This may be done during an office or lunch conference. Since we found that the jury often tries the attorney as well as his client, this step becomes compelling. (approximately one hour)

Step 4. Psychologist conducts psychological evaluation of the client. This includes observation of speech patterns, physical appearance, personality characteristics and behavioral cues to socio-economic status. Step 4 was used by psychologists for the defense in the Angela Davis case. (approximately one hour)

Step 5. Psychologist constructs ideal juror profile based on 11 factors: age, education, marital status, children, occupation, geographical background, race, religion, sex and clinical. Additional factors are included depending on the case. For example, in the Cessna case, we included the factor "frequency of air travel" and in Cundiff, "drinking behavior." Each factor can be measured on a numerical rating scale.

Each of these factors is then weighted by a predetermined multiple which reveals the amount of emphasis he places on that factor in relation to others. A juror rating sheet for each venireman is then prepared. As we approach voir dire we have an ideal profile against which each venireman will be rated on the eleven factors.

Step 6. *Voir Dire.* Since the forensic psychologist is often a member of the bar, he may sit at counsel's table. From that vantage point, he may face the jury panel and observe interactions between the attorneys, clients and the panel. During this phase, he makes his ratings and watches for cues to rapport, body language and other significant data which are elements of judgment for the factor entitled "clinical."

The psychologist prepares 11 questions for the attorney to ask which will elicit the factor information he requires. In civil cases, at least some of the information is supplied by the juror questionnaire. Of course, the attorney will want to ask questions of his own and take this opportunity to begin to present his case and clear up matters of definition such as burden of proof and comparative negligence.

Step 8.  Adjournment for strikes.  Psychologist tabulates scoring sheets and presents counsel with his recommendations for strikes. Emotionalism is removed from the process since all psychological factors are reduced to numerical measurements.  The client should be present and encouraged to contribute to the discussion.  When the client requests a strike in conflict with the psychologist, the matter should be resolved in favor of the client's opinion.

The psychology of jury selection is not hocus pocus nor should it be on an eeny meeny mini mo basis.  I am frankly critical of hypnotic and other mesmerizing approaches.  I believe that the attorney can benefit from forensic consultation for jury selection because it frees him to concentrate on presenting elements of his case during voir dire;  and his own biases which may cause him to misjudge individuals during the stress of trial are minimized.

As a psychologist I do not take credit for the victories in cases in which I have consulted.  The cases were won on the merits of the issues and by the way in which the attorneys developed and presented their evidence.  What the forensic approach did accomplish was that it struck from the jury panel those who prior to hearing the case, were predisposed to be hostile and prejudicial to the clients, their attorneys or to their cause.

## INSTRUCTIONS TO THE JURY

The legal process relies on the judge's instructions to the jury to inform and define for the jury exactly what their task is.  These may include general questions, special issues and definitions.  Often the judge looks to the attorneys to provide him with instructions which he may agree or not agree to submit.  Or the Court may write his own.  Timely exceptions to improper instructions perfect the record for later appeal.  In a personal injury case in which I consulted, the trial judge offered the jury 80 typewritten lines of instructions which he composed painstakingly and thoughtfully.  After the trial several jurors were interviewed who frankly admitted that they hadn't the foggiest idea of what the instructions meant, and that while they had asked the Court for clarification, they were still confused. More disastrous than not understanding was misunderstanding, despite the fact that jurors were allowed to take the instructions into the juryroom. In the personal injury case referred to, the instructions were by no means unique, included the following words and phrases:

| | |
|---|---|
| Burden of proof | Sustained amount |
| Preponderance of the evidence | Affirmative defense |
| Proximate cause | Allegation |
| Ordinary care | Weight and credit of evidence |
| Reasonable rate of speed | Deliberate a verdict |
| Duty of drivers | Reasonable and prudent |

Stop with an assured clear distance
Suffering detriment from omission
Contributory negligence

Instructions which define these terms often do so by reference to other legal terms which increase complexity and confusion. For insanity defenses to criminal charges, while the judge drafts sophisticated instructions in consultation with psychiatrists and psychologists, once inside the jury room, a juror often asks in his own vernacular, "Well, what do you think? Was he nuts?" From a psychological vantage point and many linguists would agree, what the juror means by "nuts" is probably not too different, however colloquial and oversimplified, from what the jurist means by "insane" and what the psychologist means by psychotic. The issue is more nebulous because some jurisdictions allow the jury to be judge of both law and fact, taking the judge's instructions as only advisory. But the jury does understand that it is their responsibility to find for one party or the other or for neither party or for the state.

Effective strategy requires that instructions include controlling fact determinations and elements of proof written straightforwardly, concisely and to the extent possible, free from legal jargon. An attorney preparing suggested instructions to the judge should have them read by laymen first in order to determine what meaning they convey to him. Research has shown that greater suggestibility results from questions that do not include personal pronouns and from those that include more than one negative. In the main, jurors take their responsibility seriously and conscientiously attempt to follow instructions when understood.

## INSIDE THE JURY ROOM

Inside the jury room, jurors set themselves to the task of selecting a foreman even without instructions to this effect by the judge, perhaps demonstrating an American preoccupation with organization. My research indicates that the foreman selection is accomplished in one of two ways. Assuming a 12 man jury and 12 chairs (Supreme Court has said 12 jurors is no longer a necessity even for capital offenses), the individual who sits at the end table position has the highest probability of being chosen. The second greatest probability of being selected goes to the individual who speaks first. Where an individual sits at the end table position and speaks first, his chances of being chosen are nearly assured.

End table positions in American culture enjoy a certain charismatic impact in the home; father traditionally sits at the end or "head" of the dinner table; in the corporation conference room, it is often reserved for the president or chairman of the board. Executives and professionals tend to take the end table positions when entering the jury room, suggesting a predisposition for authority. Passive and insecure individuals purposefully avoid it. The jury foreman's power is variable. Some jury foremen interpret their responsibility as being a moderator or chairman role; they open the topic, call for and count votes, ask the court questions on behalf of others. Others, as revealed by mock jury studies, take their selection as a mandate to rule tyrannically cutting off discussion of certain points, imposing their views, depreciating conflicting views through rigorous though not always accurate enforcement of Robert's Rules of Order.

Research indicates that females avoid end table positions (where there are 12 chairs and 11 persons already have taken places, leaving one of the ends open) they often refuse to accept the foreman responsibility. In one experimental study, a female juror was told, "You're sitting at the end, why don't you be foreman?" She responded, "No, I think it should be a man." Perhaps her reluctance was due to the connotation of the word *"foreman"* (versus *foreperson*) or because of a historical isolation of the female from the legal process. Nevertheless, it is possible to predict the jury foreman during *voir dire* with reasonable accuracy in many locales. When I presented the head of the table and first to speak rule to a rural Texas bar convention, several years ago, one country lawyer rose to his feet to disagree explaining that where he practiced, it was always the fellow who wore a tie that become the foreman.

One of the most difficult factors to predict concerning jury behavior is the interaction factor. That is how the juror will behave and react in a group situation. In group interactions otherwise aggressive individuals become passive; and passive individuals can become aggressive. Not only do the juries sometimes try the attorney, but each other, as where a disliked jury member adamantly supports a position and another thereby feels the compunction to play devil's advocate. Occasional laughter evoked by deliberating seems to enhance group cohesiveness and release tension. It does not suggest flippancy. It is functional.

Mock jury studies indicate that participants are not impressed or swayed by obvious and sophomoric emotional appeal. Such techniques often produce a boomerang effect. Appealing to fear motivation such as implying that a defendant, litigant or witness has communist sympathies, homosexual tendencies or atheistic or radical, shows disrespect for the intelligence of the jury. When one's intelligence is insulted, anger and resentfulness may develop. On the other hand, where undesirable personal character traits of an individual are apparent to the attorney they are also apparent to the jury. Jurors refuse to be brow-beaten into concluding what the attorney demands that they conclude.

A curious affectation of expertise by some jurors on the unlikely topics of law, physics and medicine has been recorded in mock courtroom studies:

Juror C: (In response to a question as to whether their verdict has to be unanimous). "Well, it's a civil jury. It has to be unanimous, otherwise it's a hung jury."

Juror E: "He (the doctor) said he found tenderness. In an ankle injury there's no tenderness."

An illustration of how so called objective testimony can lead to interpretations which are juxtaposed is revealed by the following remarks:

Juror F: "A used car salesman ought to know the kind of car he was driving."

Juror G: "He's a used car salesman, he might drive a different car home every night and not remember which is which."

Jurors also impute hostile or sinister motives to witnesses which are probably projections of their own hostile feelings.

Juror H: "I can't see sticking that guy for $6,500.00. She was going to need it (corrective shoes) anyway if she was flat-footed."

Juror I: (in response) "The father was probably standing on the corner and pushed her in."

Cultural expectations, biases and past experiences play a cogent role in attitude formation:

Juror J: "Fathers always are going to stick up for their daughters. My daughter was in an accident and was really hurt. If she wasn't, I would have stuck up for her anyway."

Juror K: "I was in an accident and you don't know how many little kids stop, look and listen in the middle of the street."

Juror L: "It was a female's estimate that he (the defendant) was going 30 miles per hour."

Juror M: "Is it possible to attain a speed of 30 miles per hour in fifteen feet, even if you had a Cadillac?"

Juror N: "I've raised several children and grandchildren and have had to frequently ask them 'Are you sure you're telling the truth?' "

## ASSESSING DAMAGES

Jurors are sensitive to requests for damages in varying amounts. No matter how serious the substance of the case, whether wrongful death or a will contest, jurors may assume an air of light headedness when deciding who gets what in civil cases. The more serious question for them is should the plaintiff recover or not. Values have always fascinated Americans and the art or cattle auction is an example of a festive suspense-filled and emotional-laden value ritual. Many Americans enjoy "shopping" for values more than the actual purchasing of consumer items. When the jury identifies with the plaintiff, a large money judgment is unconsciously paid to themselves for real and imagined wrongs over the period of a life time. Presenting values of pain and suffering, lost earning capacity and medical bills reflects the ancient concept of ancient bartering, where each party overestimates the value of his goods or service and depreciates those of the person he bargains with. Market value as a legal measure is defined as that which a leisurely buyer pays a leisurely seller at the marketplace. Other value categorizations are provided such as intrinsic value, replacement value or more objective value such as catalogue value.

Damage amounts requested create a psychological reference scale for the jury which includes anchoring points. In judging whether a person is short or tall, it makes some difference whether the observer himself is 5'6" or 6'5". In judging whether a person is heavy or light, it makes some difference whether the observer is 135 pounds or 230 pounds. When a person becomes an expert in assessing values, weights and heights, it generally means that he uses some objective reference scale other than his own internal reference system. In the case of the weight guesser at the carnival or circus, it may be as objective as a hidden scale. But when an inexperienced juror assesses damage his judgment is necessarily a subjective judgment. A $50,000 request for pain and suffering will mean different things to the juror who earns $10,000 per year when compared to the juror who earns $60,000 per year. Research indicates that people over estimate the value of damages which involve sums they are not used to dealing with. In criminal cases, a prosecutor's request that the defendant receive five years of jail time will be perceived differently by the 56 and 26-year-old juror.

The dynamics of judgment scales is illustrated by a psychological experiment performed by psychologists Wever and Zener. They presented research subjects with metal weights ranging from 84 to 100 grams. The subjects held these weights in their hands one at a time and judged whether one was heavier than the other. Each participant developed his own unconscious scale for deciding what was "light" and what was "heavy." Then the psychologists gave the participants a different series of weights ranging in weight from 92 to 108 grams. The effect of the first set of weights (84 to 100 grams) was evident since the participants judged each weight in the new series to be "heavy." Gradually the participants developed a new reference scale and weights of 92 and 93 grams began to feel "light."

Suppose that juror judgments as to value of pain and suffering in a personal injury case varied from $20,000 to $40,000. Those figures become the end points for the jury's reference scale. Suppose now that the plaintiff requests $50,000 in damages. What happens to the group reference scale?

| 20 | 25 | 30 | 35 | 40 | (Thousands of dollars) |
|----|----|----|----|----|----|
| Lo |  | Medium |  | Hi |  |

$20,000 remains a low judgment, but the medium and high anchor are shifted upwards.

| 20 | 25 | 30 | 35 | 40 | 45 | 50 |
|----|----|----|----|----|----|----|
| Lo |  |  | Medium |  |  | Hi |

When the jury is earnestly attempting to reach an "average" or "just" settlement, plaintiff has increased the perception of the average by a $5,000 increment. The jury can assimilate the $10,000 increase by adjusting their reference scale. But where the reference scale of jurors varies from $20,000 to $40,000 and plaintiff requests $100,000 damages, instead of assimilating the request, the effect is to reject the request.  The $100,000 request becomes too discrepant for assimilation.

To illustrate the point, I presented my class at Southern Methodist University with the facts of a false imprisonment suit in which I consulted.  A mother of two children had stopped at a local supermarket to pick up a half gallon of milk and a bottle of yogurt.  Since she sewed, she was attracted by a sewing display rack in the store. Seeing a zipper she wanted and because her hands were full, she draped the zipper over her purse.  Like many consumers, when she reached the checkout aisle, she decided against the purchase and put the zipper up inappropriately on some can goods.  At the counter she was grabbed by an over-zealous assistant manager who threw her bodily into his office in view of her children.  He held her incommunicado for one hour while he cross-examined her and refused to let her go to the rest room.  He then called the police who arrested her, booked her, and locked her in a jail cell.  As a result of this experience, the woman developed acute anxiety attacks for which I treated her.   Each student received the fact situation but half the students (Group I) were told the plaintiff sought $20,000 in damages. The other half (Group II) were told the plaintiff sought $500,000 in damages.  All students were told they could award, if they found the store negligent, any amount of money they thought just.  Apparently the class reference scale average hovered at about $20,000. The $500,000 request to Group II was completely rejected by that group.   They gave an average award of $10,000 in damages with many voting $1.00.

In assessing nominal, actual and exemplary damages, group influence exerts a powerful influence on unagreeable jurors by imposing majority judgments.  Many lawyers during *voir dire* consider only the venireman in isolation and overlook his potential role in a group decision.  Psychologist Solomon Asch, asked research subjects to choose a comparison line which matched a standard line in length. A simple enough task.

(Adapted from the Asch Line Experiment.)

STANDARD                    COMPARISONS

Eight subjects sat in a group as the lines were presented on a blackboard for comparison. Seven of the eight were confederates of Professor Asch and were instructed to always choose the wrong line. Pressures to conform were so compelling that even when all objective cues pointed otherwise, 32% of the subjects tested erred in the direction of the majority.

This chapter exposes generalities and myths which have reduced the effectiveness of attorneys during *voir dire*. An empirical approach which includes the analysis of approximately ten psychological and demographic factors is explained. For the first time, the attorney as well as the client is studied for potential jury impact. This system does not have the mystery of the hypnotic approach but is straightforward, easily adapted and has been effective in both criminal and civil cases. Having observed many jury trials and conducted research on jury decision making, the author concludes that jurors are serious and conscientious, and genuinely seek justice. The challenge for the trial lawyer is to keep those who are biased from serving on a jury. Forensic psychology can help in this effort.

In the next chapter, *"View From the Bench,"* we will look at the judge's psychological as well as legal predispositions to make decisions.

# chapter 5

# View from the Bench

Montanir 75

A district judge confided:

The plaintiff was urging a legal rule which you thought was wrong. I thought it was legally right, but very unjust, and I didn't want to apply it. So, I made up my mind to lick the plaintiff on the facts. And by giving him every break on procedural points, I made it impossible for him to reverse me on appeal, because as the testimony was oral and in conflict, I knew the upper court would never upset my findings. [39]

The purpose of this chapter is to attempt to understand the judicial experience and the psychological factors which affect judicial decision making. These cogent factors are often masked by the rules of federal and state procedure and by *stare decisis*, which gives both direction and relief from the private agonizing of sole decision making of district judges. The district judge sits where the action is, and he cannot afford the luxury of taking every motion or objection under advisement while a law clerk searches for a recent opinion. When groups of men make appellate decisions, a different set of psychological rules apply.

There are 89 Federal District Courts, 10 Circuit Courts of Appeal, in addition to the United States Supreme Court. Each state has its own complex judicial system. In Texas, there are over 200 State District Courts, 14 Courts of Civil Appeal, 1 Court of Criminal Appeals, and a State Supreme Court. In addition, there are special federal courts such as the courts of tax, claims, customs and patent, and special state courts such as domestic relations and juvenile courts. Salaries for judges may range from $18,600 to $62,500. Most judges are appointed, but then also face election. Supreme Court Justices, once appointed, serve for life pending good behavior.

39. Frank, J. COURTS ON TRIAL. Princeton U. Press: 1949, Princeton, N.J., p. 168.

## PATIENCE AND TOLERANCE

Unlike his appellate colleagues, the district judge sees and digests the courtroom drama, its climax, anti-climax and boredom. The effective trial judge must be tolerant and patient. While waiting to testify as to whether a citizen had been emotionally coerced into yielding tax records, I observed two lawyers arguing a motion before a Federal Judge. One of the young lawyers spoke with an animated, confident voice. But the judge became perceptibly fidgety as the lawyer droned on. He began shuffling papers and scratched his head. Finally, he interrupted the young man and bellowed, "Mr. Frank, I can't follow your brief—where are you arguing from." The lawyer looked palely at his brief and stammered, "Oh my God, your honor, I have just argued a similar motion in Florida and I'm reading from the wrong brief." The judge looked skyward.

But events and feelings of the judge can puncture stability and calm, and lead to angry, and sometimes unstable responses. This is most readily a result of breaking or changing the rules of courtroom conduct into which a judge may retreat to for safety and direction. In 1969, eight men were accused of conspiring to riot at the Chicago Democratic Convention. The defendants refused to follow the rules of the court. The defendant, Seale, refused to stand as the learned Judge Julius Hoffman entered the Court. He hurled invectives at the Judge: "Fascist pig, imperialist, *oink, oink, oink!*" Defendant disruptions can be handled by three means: threatening contempt, sending the defendant from the courtroom, or gagging and shackling. In an impulse of anger, Judge Hoffman ordered the defendant gagged and shackled before an international press which, in the eyes of some jurist observers, did more harm than good.

An example of judicial anger which lead to a thoughtful response erupted in a child custody suit for which I was asked to advise the court. A grandfather, acting as his own attorney, sued his son and daughter-in-law for custody of their 18-month-old child. The plaintiff's evidence of abuse to support a change of custody was a documented case of diaper rash. He subpoenaed the child's pediatrician, who exclaimed on the stand; "No doubt about it, the kid's got diaper rash." When the plaintiff asked his wife whether she believed the child loved her more than the child's mother, the court interrupted:

> *Court:* "I'm not going to allow that question. My soul—an 18-month-old child, and you're going to ask somebody who the child loves most? Let's move on."

On direct examination, the daughter-in-law expressed fear of the plaintiff, so on cross examination he asked her, "When did you first become afraid of me?" She answered, "When you knocked me to the ground." "On what date?" inquired the plaintiff meekly. When he refused to connect an irrelevant line of questioning which he promised the court he would tie together, he proceeded to walk out of the courtroom.

> *Court:* "Hold on, counsel. Come back and sit down. If you are going to be counsel you don't have the prerogative to leave until the Court is dismissed."
> *Plaintiff:* "Your Honor, may I go to the restroom?"
> *Court:* "No sir, not until I dismiss the Court. This whole matter is sick. Get with something, or I'm going to dismiss the the case and we're going to get into something that needs the Court's time. This courtroom will not be a place where people with animosity toward each other cut each other to pieces just because they can't get along. I haven't heard anything directly concerned with the little baby and what's best for the baby's future."

## VARIABILITY OF JUDICIAL BEHAVIOR

In an exhaustive study of the New Jersey judiciary[40] for an average number of cases, one judge was observed to have given almost twice as many penal sentences as his colleagues for similar of-

---

40. F. Gaudett, "Individual Differences in the Sentencing Tendencies of Judges," ARCHIVES OF PSYCHOLOGY, 1938, Volume 32, pp. 5-57.

fenses. In an early study conducted by Professor Burtt,[41] an experimental psychologist, penal sentences by judges in a large metropolitan area were found to peak at 5, 10, 15, 20 and 25 years. Shorter sentences peaked at 1, 3, 6 and 9 months. In still another metropolitan study, out of 880 penal sentences surveyed, Burtt discovered that 360 were for 3 years, 60 for 4 years, 240 for 5 years and 20 were for 6 years. It is problematic that such a large number of convicted offenders could deserve 3 or 5 year sentences as opposed to 4 or 6 year terms. These studies indicate a compelling need for prospective judges to undergo training in handing down sentences. There is a current trend for giving judges time off during the summer to attend institutes and conferences which explore the decision making process.

University of Chicago Law Professor Hans Zeisel[42] reported that over a 20 year period, there was a marked discrepancy in judge's capital punishment sentences for rape offenses as a function of race in Cook County, Illinois,

|  | Blacks convicted of raping white women | All other convicted rapists |
| --- | --- | --- |
| % of cases where defendant was sentenced to death | 46% | 14% |

The category, "all other convicted rapists," consisted of black men convicted of raping black women, and white men convicted of raping white women. There were no cases found where a white man was convicted of raping a black woman. This becomes especially disturbing since Anglo—American law requires judges to explain decisions as to guilt or innocence, but they are not required to explain sentences which fall between a maximum and minimum set by statute.

Professor Zeisel also investigated the relationship between characteristics of criminal defendants, their victims, situational crime

---

41. H. Burtt, LEGAL PSYCHOLOGY, Prentice Hall, Inc., New York, 1931.
42. H. Zeisel, LAW & SOCIETY RIVIEW, 1969, Volume 3, pp. 621-631.

factors, and the frequency of death sentences rendered. A list of salient factors involved in predicting sentence severity is provided below, recognizing that capital punishment is rarely effected.


## FACTORS AFFECTING PENAL SENTENCES

1. age of defendant
2. mental status of the defendant
3. whether defendant has dependent children
4. whether defendant has prior convictions
5. possible prison record of defendant
6. age of victim
7. whether victim has dependent children
8. place of offense
9. illegal entry to place of offense
10. display of weapons
11. seriousness of injury to victim
12. whether victim was a stranger
13. whether defendant pleaded guilty
14. quality of counsel (appointed or hired)

Variability in the attitude of judges listed in the *Directory of American Judges* was investigated by social scientist, Stuart Nagel. Strong agreement and disagreement, with various attitude positions are reproduced below:

| ITEM | DISAGREEMENT | AGREEMENT |
|------|--------------|-----------|
| laws favor the rich | 35% | 3% |
| abandon some sovereignty | 22% | 10% |
| spare rod, spoil child | 6% | 18% |
| go back to religion | 7% | 25% |
| colored are inferior | 13% | 8% |
| premartial sex permissible | 38% | 2% |
| have equal pay for both sexes | 4% | 14% |

In *Berger vs. United States,* Mr. Justice McReynolds observed: "An amorphous dummy, unspotted by human emotions [is not] a becoming receptacle for judicial power." Obviously, the fact that judges experience bias is not as important as is their ability and willingness to recognize their bias and seek to control it. In *NLRB vs. Pittsburgh S. S. Co.,* an administrative agency examiner found all company witnesses to be untrustworthy, and all union witnesses to be reliable. The NLRB accepted without reservation the examiner's determination showed undue bias. The Supreme Court reversed the holding, stating: "total rejection of an opposed view cannot, of itself, impugn the integrity or competence of a trier of fact." Professor Kenneth Culp Davis, in his treatise on Administrative Law, differentiates several categories of judicial bias: bias about issues, facts, parties and interest.

A judge's experience has been shown to have a statistically significant relation to his acquittal record, as illustrated by a Chicago study reported by Law Professors Kalven and Zeisel.

### THE JUDGE'S BACKGROUND AND ACQUITTAL RATE

| BACKGROUND | NUMBER OF CASES | ACQUITTAL |
|---|---|---|
| Former prosecutor | 482 | 13% |
| Former defense counsel | 449 | 22% |
| Neither or both | 1396 | 16% |
| The jury | 2327 | 33% |

A recent trend in sentencing in criminal cases recognizes the futility of the age-old method of punishment by the time clock. A few courts are breaking new ground in dealing with individuals guilty of crimes against property and against persons. A Phoenix, Arizona doctor was found guilty of illegally selling amphetamines. Instead of life imprisonment, he was sentenced to seven years of practicing medicine in Tombstone, Arizona, which did not have a doctor of its own. Judge Samuel Zoll of Salem, Massachusettes sentences a juvenile who turns in a false fire alarm to 80 hours of polishing fire engines. For slashing trees, Judge Zoll metes out a sentence of 40 hours of planting seedlings in town parks. But not everyone will agree that justice is done. When Bertha Costos killed her husband with a butcher knife, a Dade County Judge sentenced her to five years of teaching Sunday school or fifteen years in jail. Also, some criminals seem to prefer prison to rehabilitation. Another Florida citizen chose a two year prison term to spending several years teaching black children how to read.[43] Having had himself committed to a state prison for research purposes, Foster Furcolo, a former Masschusetts governor concluded: "Every evaluation and analysis ever made of any prisoner proves that he would be better off anyplace except where he is—morally, spiritually, financially, or by any other standard.[44]

## THE BLACK ROBE

The concentration of power exists in individuals appointed or elected to a judgeship. There is procedural power to subpoena records and to compel testimony. There is control over the conduct of attorneys and litigants who are unwilling to abide by the rules of evidence. There is power to direct and to set aside verdicts. The Supreme Court has the power to decide the constitutionality of legislative and executive acts, thereby checking the power of elected officials. A cogent example of Supreme Court powers is the Court's 1974 decision to compel President Richard Nixon to produce for inspection tape recordings of his private conversation.

Sociological studies of status and occupational preference indicate that members of the Supreme Court enjoy the greatest reverence and admiration of any other member in society. Following Supreme Court Justices in prestige are heart surgeons, the president, and other professionals. This prestige compliments an already awesome power. Lord Acton observed: "The power corrupts, and absolute power corrupts absolutely." Most psychologists concur. Individuals who seek judgeship are predictively those who possess high ego strength. High ego strength is necessary to live with day to day

43. NEWSWEEK, December 23, 1974,
44. COURT, Volume X, June, 1970.

decisions which affect individual freedom, property and the well-being of others.

Reflecting on the Judge's authority, Dallas, Texas Judge Oswin Chrisman reflects; "The power is tantalizing, but sinful. In all honesty, when you walk into a room and everybody stands, it has an effect. This, in my opinion, is a major pitfall of the judiciary." Judge Fran Goodwin observes: "I love to have my own way in court or around the house, but I don't feel authoritarian on the bench. I love the responsibility of making decisions, but I'm dead serious when fooling with someone's liberty." Court of Civil Appeals Justice Clarence Guittard observes that "playing God," or the abuse of judicial power is dependent upon particular cases. In his view, persons who lose a case tend to question a judge's ability, and suspect abuse of power. However, he notes, "In court the judge has overall authority. He has power, and everyone else is at his mercy. There must be safeguards, because the court should be run for the people; but in particular cases it may be run for the interest of the judge."

Former Texas Supreme Court Justice Robert Hamilton once declared, "I believe it is true in some cases that judges 'play God.' This is especially true of trial judges, but less often true of appellate judges who do not make individual decisions, but group decisions where their own opinions are matched against the opinions of other judges."

There is psychological evidence for Judge Guittard's position that perception of abuse of power is related to a negative outcome for a litigant or defendant. Psychologist Muzafer Sherif designed a study of Perception Fairness of the Judge by a Losing Group:

cf
sp.r—
p 109

> A neutral outsider was brought in as a judge for intergroup experiments. Both sides agreed initially that the third party was Neutral and competent. Groups subsequently awarded the decision continued to rate the judge as neutral and competent, taking his decision as evidence of their merit and good performance. Losing groups, on the other hand, no longer saw

the judge as neutral. Their ratings were that he was "biased, unfair, and incompetent." They criticized him for showing "no grasp of the problem," for "not knowing enough about the topic," for "not being intelligent enough to be fair and unbiased," and for "not taking enough time to arrive at a fair decision." [45]

The attorney who transgresses the judge's prerogatives and challenges his authority in an obvious and overt way should not be surprised when the judge consciously or unconsciously punishes him. In federal courts it may amount to an unfavorable comment on the weight of the evidence. In an administrative proceeding it may take the form of rendering an unfavorable decision without further explanation. In a state court, the judge's feelings may manifest themselves in the form of an untimely recess during a star witness' testimony.

What are the status coordinates of a judge's power and prestige? They are contextual. The judge's physical interpersonal space is protected from penetration by a large wooden podium type structure, and his seat is elevated several steps higher than the jury box and the litigants' tables. His honorific title, "Your Honor," differentiates him from other participants in court, reinforced by his black garb suggesting solemnity, gravity, sobriety, and even religiosity. He is recipient of one of the highest honors in American society—a private parking place. So great is the charisma coincident with the judicial role, that long after the mysterious disappearance of New York's Justice Crater, controversy persisted because of the seeming incongruity of a judge's voluntary absence from his job without explanation.

## EXPRESSIONS AND GESTURES

A trial judge speaks infrequently during the course of the trial. When he does, it is generally to provide instruction to the

---

45. From SOCIAL PSYCHOLOGY, M. Sherif, 1956, p. 264.

jury, or to rule on motion and points of evidence. Almost never does the judge indulge himself to the extent that he expresses his personal, as opposed to juridical, opinion regarding the drama unfolding before him. Gestures which a judge makes while talking and his postural position while hearing testimony will provide the attorney, as well as the casual observer, with cues as to how a judge is reacting.

*Frustration*

*Boredom*

*Evaluation*

*Exhaustion*

*Contemplation*

*Negative Reaction*

## APPELLATE ATTITUDE CHANGE

*cf sp. on p. 106*

Dr. (Mustafer) Sherif has accomplished exciting breakthroughs in the area of attitude assessment and change. His social-psychological analyses are vital tools for the practicing attorney. Sherif divides attitudes held by an individual into three "latitudes," or areas of measurement:  the latitude of acceptance, the latitude of rejection, and the latitude of non-commitment. The latitude of acceptance includes a judge's own private attitude on a particular legal issue such as:  an individual has an affirmative duty not to breach contracts; proximate cause should include direct results of negligence; realistic, though emotionally loaded photographs can be shown to juries. While these statements represent the judge's own attitudes, other attitudinal positions are also acceptable.  For example, there are some circumstances which will justify breaching a contract; proximate cause may include indirect consequences of negligence; realistic, though emotionally loaded photographs can be shown to juries when essential to the case. A diagram of the latitude approach, where each number represents an attitudinal position, is graphically illustrated below:

### ANALYSIS OF A JUDGE'S ATTITUDE POSITIONS

| Acceptance | Non-commitment | Rejection |
|:---:|:---:|:---:|
| 12345678 | 123 | 12345 |

The latitude of non-commitment represents attitudinal positions which the judge neither wholly accepts nor rejects. His feelings about them are ambivalent.  The latitude of rejection includes attitudes which the judge categorically rejects.  The rejection latitude might include the following statements:  Since they represent products of a capitalistic society, contracts can be broken at the convenience of either party; only indirect damages should be considered in evaluating damages resulting from proximate cause; realistic, though emotionally loaded photographs must never be submitted to the jury.

The meaning of the latitude analysis for persuasion and attitude change on appeal is set out by Sherif:

> ...If the person is susceptible to change at all, communications advocating positions within his latitudes of acceptance or non-commitment will produce the greatest change, while communications advocating positions within his latitude of rejection will either produce no change or, if they are sufficiently discrepant, will result in change away from the communication.[46]

This means that once the attorney has isolated the attitude most nearly representative of a current or preceding court's case law position involving similar facts, the most effective legal argument will be a position close enough to a judge's "own" position that it can be assimilated into the "own" position. Argument which falls into the category of non-commitment would also be acceptable. Legal arguments aid the judge in rationalizing and supporting a decision in favor of the argument. The danger of presenting an argument widely discrepant from a judge's own position, especially under conditions of strong ego involvement, has a boomerang effect.

The attorney may nevertheless feel compelled because of factual limitations, or because of conflicting psycho-legal factors (such as the client's expectations and needs), to assume an argument position which would predictably fall in the court's latitude of rejection. When this is the case, is should be remembered that when an individual is known to be opposed to a position, two-sided, versus one-sided communication is always more persuasive. Although this contradicts legal proclivity for an adversary approach, presenting your opponent's argument and its rational conclusion before your own (when it falls in the rejection range), will make the latter more acceptable. This approach is particularly useful when the judge feels very strongly about his position—when he is ego-involved. Here fewer positions are acceptable.

---

46. Sherif, M., OUTLINE OF SOCIAL PSYCHOLOGY, 1964.

## LATITUDES UNDER
## EGO-INVOLVEMENT CONDITIONS

| Acceptance | Non-commitment | Rejection |
|:---:|:---:|:---:|
| 123 | 1234 | 123456789 |

During oral argument, the effective attorney is aware of the fact that communication includes feedback. His effectiveness is magnified when he is able to receive and decode the judge's messages of interest, lethargy, boredom, emotion of acceptance or rejection. Facial expression, body positioning, and eye movement are barometers of emotional effect, and not as likely to deceive as voice patterns. Communications can be altered or modified according to how they are being received. Frequently an attorney, disregarding fatal signs of boredom, anger, or rejection, insists on presenting all 13 points scribbled on his note pad, despite indications that he's not going over too well. Under these circumstances, the effective attorney states his points quickly, and then gropes for a different tack. In psychotherapy, the psychologist sends cues to his patient through a disapproving or approving glance, or verbalization, such as an *"uh-huh."* The attorney receives similar cues from the appellate justices, although these cues are sometimes more subtle.

*View From The Bench* indicates the need for a new perspective of the judge, his expectations, his motivation, emotional and personality characteristics. The judge is a man who dons a robe, carries a gavel, and has a particular professional job to do for the community. No other charismatic qualities emerge merely by virtue of being appointed or elected a judge. His attitudes and judgments are amenable to the same psychological analysis as other individuals, and the attorney who understands and appreciates this idea maximizes his chances for effective interaction with the judge.

# chapter 6

# How Evidence Is Perceived

Montañés 74

"Place your right hand on the Bible. Do you swear to tell the truth, the whole truth and nothing but the truth so help you God?"

At common law, an oath was mandatory before testimony of a witness would be received in court and each witness was required to kiss the Bible. Testimony of atheists was excluded at the court's discretion because its veracity was believed suspect. Psychologist Edwin Boring scientifically studied the effect of oath taking. He discovered that when men were asked to testify about evidence without first taking an oath to tell the truth errors increased 1.8 times. For women not under oath, errors in testimony were even greater. Testimony of children was found to be laden with inaccuracies, exaggerations and distortions whether or not an oath was administered.[47]

This year, I consulted on the preparation of an appellant's brief for a defendant who was found guilty of perjury. He was accused of having lied under oath to a federal grand jury when he denied having placed five phone calls during a four month period, four years prior to his allegedly perjured testimony. The phone calls involved a $230,000 transaction between the defendant and a third party. The defendant admitted the transaction but stated he could not recall the five ancillary conversations about it. As he was a commodity broker, telephone records indicated he had placed 8,000 phone calls between the time the five calls were placed and his grand jury testimony. Was he lying or did he simply forget? The appellant's brief set out psychological studies of memory, cognitive interference, meaningfulness of the event recalled and the nature of questions which elicit recall. These studies supported the defense of forgetting. The appellate court has not yet ruled.

## PRINCIPLES OF PERCEPTION

The first witness for the defense or prosecution, plaintiff or

47. E. Boring, Journal of the American Institute of Criminal Law, 1916, Vol. 6, p. 820.

114

defendant, has the greatest opportunity for attitude persuasion and impact on the jury or judge because the first witness creates a "set" or standard by which later testimony is evaluated and compared. "Set" is a readiness or predisposition to respond to a word, sight, smell or sound in a particular way. For example, if an individual is told that he is about to see a rapid presentation of a word projected on a screen, how he perceives that word depends on what he is prepared to see. This principle is called "synesthesia."

Psychologist E. M. Sipola[48] presented two groups of individuals with words flashed on a screen at a high rate of speed (10 hundredths of a second per flash). Group I was instructed that they were about to see words relating to animals. Group II was told that they were about to see words that involved travel or transportation. The words themselves had nothing to do with animals or travel. They were actually nonsense words—words without meaning. A significant number of persons in both groups reported seeing words in the direction of the set or cues given. When the nonsense word "pasrot" was presented, Group I members reported seeing "parrot;" Group II members saw the word "passport."

| Nonsense Word | What Group I Saw | What Group II Saw |
| --- | --- | --- |
| chack | chick | check |
| sae | seal | sail |
| wharl | whale | wharf |
| pasrot | parrot | passport |
| dack | duck | deck |
| pengion | penguin | pension |

The set phenomenon can be observed for memory of shapes and forms as well as words. This is especially true where the shape is ambiguous or confusing. The central application of set for the attorney on cross examination is the realization that witnesses to a contract, will, accident or crime, will see what they are prepared to see.

 bottle or stirrup?         table or hour glass?

seven or four?        sun or ship's wheel?

 broom or gun?

**48.** E. Sipola, PSYCHOLOGICAL MONOGRAPHS, 1935, 46 number 210.

## THE SET PHENOMENON

When a person is emotionally disturbed, a psychological set or readiness to see or interpret events in a particular way can lead to violence. Several years ago, a patient was referred to me who had, by his own admission, killed his aunt. The patient, who farmed for a living, believed his aunt who had criticized him in the past intended to do him harm. Suffering from paranoia, he responded with typical paranoid ideation—"This person intends to kill me, so I had better kill her first." The patient was found to be insane at the time of the trial and committed to the Texas facility for the criminally insane. When rehabilitated, he will stand trial for the crime itself. When asked why he killed her, the patient answered:

"Well, it bothers me. I try not to think about it, and then I just thought what would happen if I didn't. My whole family would have been gone. I have had a battle with myself about whether to go hunting again."

The mind has unique organizational abilities which code information as to avoid redundancy. By studying these abilities, confusing and contradictory testimony is often unraveled. Suppose a witness is asked to describe the dots below:

He will not testify to having seen 21 individual dots. Rather he sees and reports them as 7 columns of 3 dots or 3 rows of 7 dots. Such mental coding is more than a memory technique since individuals actually see the rows and dots. The coding takes place in the nervous system at the higher cortical levels of the brain.

Judges and jurors often complain about hours of relentless testimony which emphasize again and again a particular statement or idea such as shareholders of a corporation not having notice of the meeting which led to a contested consolidation, or that the corporation president had no authority to contract for over $100,000 worth of goods or services without the express approval of the Board of Directors. Curiously, repetition of testimony fixates repeated information in memory, whether the testimony is true or false. A point of diminishing returns may be reached when the recipient of the information becomes so exasperated from sheer monotony that he minimizes the significance of the information since he had adapted to it. In a mock jury trial of a personal injury case which I conducted, one juror responded during deliberation:

> "At first I was sympathetic to the little girl. But after listening to her attorney talking and talking about all that hurting, I became numb."

Because of court congestion and subsequent delay, alterations in testimony of witnesses should be expected. When not expected, many an attorney becomes embarrassed and chagrined on the examination of his own witness. To reduce this possibility, most attorneys attempt to take depositions as soon after the incident, injury or crime as possible. Through reading and reviewing depositions or personal notes, ultimate testimony becomes based on memory of the deposition, not the original incident. This change makes testimony more vulnerable to attack since its direction is to more symmetrical, meaningful and credible reporting. One district attorney I know of, has been successful in interviewing witnesses by telephone. He then refers to their telephone statements on cross examination for the purpose of impeachment. Without his presence or a stenographer's, he is able to elicit less guarded and more informative answers to his questions.

What is the nature of the two figures below?

The casual observer will say, "a circle and a square, not fully formed or closed." Since the figures are not closed, they cannot geometrically qualify as a circle and a square. After a month's time, most observers remember them only as a square and a circle and forget the "not fully formed" feature. Whether a car door was closed or slightly opened immediately before an accident, or whether a window was securely fastened or opened slightly, has made the difference between a defendant or plaintiff prevailing in a law suit. Witnesses have the tendency to recall only those facets of what they observed which make sense. They tend to overlook and forget events which contradict or confuse their percept.

A noteworthy feature of courtroom testimony is its lack of reliability and validity, regardless of the witnesses' good faith or sinister motivation for accuracy. The effective attorney recognizes that distortions and inaccuracies often follow a predictable pattern. Forensic psychologist Hugo Munsterberg[49] reported a case in which it became pertinent to determine the approximate number of persons involved in a riot. Some witnesses swore there could not have been more than 20 persons present. Others were equally convinced they saw over 100. In 1962 on the grassy knoll opposite the Texas Schoolbook Depository, hundreds of persons witnessed the assassination of President Kennedy. Many reported having heard shots fired. Some reported a single shot; and others insisted there were three to five shots fired. Some said the shots came from the depository; some were convinced the shots came from the direction of the knoll; some reported seeing shadowing figures, and others reported suspicious persons fleeing toward downtown. A simple experiment on the time duration between sounds necessary for the sounds to be perceived separately and distinctly, correlated with the time frames of the Zapruder film would shed light on the continuing mystery.

For a personal injury case in which I consulted, a critical fact issue involved determining whether a train whistle was sounded as a trucker drove his car across the railroad tracks. The impact resulted in an explosion which killed the driver and several other motorists. The plaintiff suing for wrongful death claimed there was no whistle sounded. One witness claimed the train whistle was loud and clear. Another witness recalled a sound preceding the tragic accident but doubted it was a whistle. Who was lying and who was telling the truth? Could both witnesses have been telling the truth?

---

49. H. Munsterberg, ON THE WITNESS STAND, Clark Boardman Co., New York, 1923.

Dr. Hugo Munsterberg once asked 100 students to concentrate on a sound he would produce in class, then to identify and describe it. Hidden from view, he struck a tuning fork from behind his lectern. Only two students correctly identified the sound. Others judged it to be a bell, organ pipe, muffled gong, horn, cello string or violin. To some, it sounded like a lion's growl, a steam whistle, fog horn or human voice. Descriptions of tonal quality included: soft, rough, mellow, sharp, humming, whistling, solemn, resonant, penetrating, full, rumbling, clear and low.

The lack of perceptual reliability is also revealed in police line-up identification. Researchers Buckhout, Alper et al.[50] staged a purse snatching incident in a Brooklyn college classroom. Student eyewitnesses were asked to describe the assailant. Three weeks later, the eyewitnesses were shown videotaped lineups of five persons. The actual assailant was not included, but another individual with similar physical characteristics was. Twenty-nine percent of the witnesses chose the look alike, 19 percent were unable to make an identification and 44 percent picked the wrong man entirely.

Attention to principles of perceptual organization won acquittal for an English defendant accused of sexual perversion based on the testimony from forensic psychologist Dr. L. R. C. Haward. Two police officers had concealed themselves in a broom closet of a public bathroom for a period of a week and arrested two men in flagrante delicto. The defendant maintained that the protruding end of his pink scarf was mistaken for his penis by the officers. The psychologist reconstructed the event and photographed the two men in various positions. The photographs were shown to 12 adults under various conditions of light, exposure time, and degree of expectancy that the particular picture illustrated an indecent act. In 1440 exposures, only 413 were perceived as mutual masturbation. When the illumination and exposure time were most identical to that involved in the alleged offense, only one photograph in 8 was perceived as portraying indecency. Since the 12% probability of error was considered a "reasonable doubt" as to what occurred, the case was dismissed.

50. R. Buckhout, A. Alper, S. Chern, G. Silverberg & M. Slomovits, EYEWITNESS IDEN-FICATION, Social Action and the Law Newsletter, Vol. 1, Number 4, 1974.

Perceptual distortions and adaptations occur in all sense modalities, not just vision.  Dr. Gregory[51] notes that after carrying a heavy weight for a few minutes, an individual's arm tends to feel lighter and may rise a few inches of its own volition.  Temperature is also variable.  Take three bowls of water, one filled with hot water, one filled with warm water and one filled with cold water.  Immerse one hand in the hot water and the other hand in the cold water for five minutes.  Then simultaneously place both hands in the warm water.  The "hot water" hand will feel cold.  The "cold water" hand will feel hot.

## PRESTIGE SUGGESTION

Prestige suggestion has a definite and measurable effect on the development of attitudes.  In one psychological study, a well dressed gentleman in a fashionable suit, top hat and walking cane was placed at a busy metropolitan intersection.  It was prearranged that he would wait until the traffic light signaled "Don't Walk" and then proceed to jaywalk against the light.  As he stepped off the curb a significant number of pedestrians waiting for the light to change joined the "gentleman" in crossing against the light.  The condition was duplicated a second time in which the "gentleman" was dressed as a skid row "derelict."  As the "derelict" stepped off the curb to cross against the light, he did so alone. Another study of prestige suggestion proved that charitable contributions could be increased by first presenting prospective donors with a list of prominent philanthropists who have already contributed.

Dr. Paul Jacobs, consultant to the Dallas Police Department, and I studied the effect of prestige suggestion on perception of guilt in a criminal case.  A script of a store burglary was composed and presented to university students.  After reading the fact summary, each student was asked to consider himself a mock juror and state whether the defendant was guilty or innocent.  The scripts were altered to reflect a high or low prestige address for the defendant. For example, the high prestige address was 48 Executive Arms Apartments.  The low prestige address was 5107 W. 35th Street. A significant number of mock jurors whose fact summary included the high prestige address believed the defendant innocent.  An op-

---

51. R. Gregory, EYE AND BRAIN, World University Library, New York, 1966.

posite effect was recorded for the low prestige condition.

Prestige suggestion enters the legal process most directly in the form of the expert witness when properly qualified. In suits involving the sale of real property, anti-trust suits as well as insanity pleas, both sides typically present one or more experts. Testimony of experts is often contradictory. It is commonly believed that such witnesses cancel each other out. Nevertheless, some experts are more articulate, convincing and prestigious than others. To illustrate how mental health professionals are affected by prestige suggestion, Professor Maurice Temerlin[52] taped a diagnostic interview with a patient who was actually a hired actor reading from a script. The script was written to reflect a healthy, normal personality who enjoyed his work, reacted warmly to the doctor, was confident, identified with the same sex parent and loved his wife. A group of psychologists and psychiatrists listened to the tape and were asked to make a diagnosis. Before their evaluations, each group was told that an eminent member of their profession had said that the patient "looked neurotic, but was actually quite psychotic." The "mentally healthy" patient was diagnosed as normal by only three experts.

## PERCEPTION OF GUILT AND NEGLIGENCE

Some judges and attorneys stress the importance of facial characteristics and other somatic factors as indicating the validity of testimony. In *Quercia vs. United States*[53] the defendant, convicted on a narcotics charge, was put on the witness stand. On appeal, he asserted that the trial judge's allusion to his demeanor constituted reversible error. The judge's instructions included:

"I'm going to tell you what I think of the defendant's testimony. You may have noticed Mr. Foreman and Gentlemen, that he wiped his hands during his testimony. It is a rather curious thing, but that is almost always an indication of lying. Why it should be so, we don't know, but that is the fact. I think that every single word that he said, except when he agreed with the Government's testimony, was a lie."

52. M. Temerlin, JOURNAL OF NERVOUS AND MENTAL DISEASE, Volume 147, pp. 349–353.
53. Quercia vs. United States 289. V.S. 466.

Increased anxiety and tension are associated with purposeful lying because of guilt, fear of being discovered or excitement in duping others. Increased tension through the action of the sympathetic nervous system increases sweating and trembling. The judge's comments were invalid because some individuals, particularly the socio-pathic personality do not become anxious when lying or committing criminal acts. I asked one socio-pathic and schizoid youngster whom I evaluated at the Dallas juvenile detention center, "How did you feel when you brandished your gun at the store clerk?" He answered, "It was exhilarating." More importantly, increased sweating does not allow for directional analysis. Was the defendant anxious because he was purposely misrepresenting the truth, or because he was telling the truth but thought he wouldn't be believed?

A variety of somatic complaints were reported by American pilots flying combat missions in World War II.[54]

## SOMATIC COMPLAINTS OF COMBAT PILOTS

Pounding heart and rapid pulse
Muscles very tense
Easily irritated, angry or "sore"
Dryness of the throat or mouth
"Nervous perspiration" or "cold sweat"
"Butterflies" in the stomach
Sense of unreality, that this couldn't be happening
Need to urinate frequently
Trembling
Confused or rattled
Weak or faint
After mission, not being able to remember details of
     what happened
Sick to the stomach
Not being able to concentrate

Somatic experiences described by the combat pilots are not identified with flying air craft under perilous conditions alone. Trial lawyers during case preparation may also experience one or more of these symptoms. Emotional experience often correlates with, induces or causes somatic complaints.

---

54. L. Schaffer, FEAR AND COURAGE IN AERIAL COMBAT, Journal of Consulting Psychology, Volume II, 1947, pp. 137—143.

The human nervous system is composed of two branches: the central nervous (brain and spinal column) and the autonomic. The central nervous system controls rational mental processes: perception, thinking, and ideating. But it is the autonomic branch which exerts the most cogent influence over emotional response. The autonomic is differentiated into sympathetic and parasympathetic functions. The former usually exhibits a stimulating effect on internal organs as in increasing heart beat or the secretion of endocrine hormones, while the latter has an inhibitory effect such as the cessation of digestion and salivary secretions.

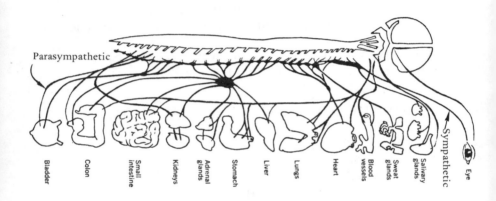

Parasympathetic — Sympathetic

Bladder · Colon · Small intestine · Kidneys · Adrenal glands · Stomach · Liver · Lungs · Heart · Blood vessels · Sweat glands · Salivary glands · Eye

## THE AUTONOMIC NERVOUS SYSTEM [55]

The autonomic nervous system prepares the individual for an emergency because it enlarges the blood vessels serving exterior muscles of the body (the arms and legs); increases heart rate, glucose or sugar content in the blood; and induces the secretion of adrenalin. Such glandular and metabolic changes contribute to the almost super human effort reported in cases where fathers single-handedly lifted cars in order to free a trapped child, or where one jumps a great distance to avoid being crushed by a falling object.

The polygraph or lie detector test, often used in criminal investigations measured changes in heart beat, respiration and galvanic skin response. The theory is that these functions will increase in intensity when one is lying. Under the directions of untrained operators, the polygraph is often misunderstood and its results

55. Morgan and King, INTRODUCTION TO PSYCHOLOGY, 1966, p. 254.

misapplied. The polygraph does not indicate when a subject is lying; it only indicates that strong emotionality is elicited by particular stimulus questions. The same critical words, "store, 11:00 p.m., gun, cash register, shooting, get away," might elicit the same or similar autonomic changes in the armed robber as in the two or three witnesses, innocent of the crime, but who saw the robbery. Notwithstanding, ataraxic or tranquilizing drugs mask, confound and confuse lie detector results — a fact which most experienced law breakers know.

A less confusing indice of emotional response is the measurement of pupil dilation. As light rays enter the eye and strike the layer of photosensitive receptors, the pupils adjust by contracting or expanding. University of Chicago psychologist Hess discovered quite by accident that his eyes seemed to vacillate between dilation and contraction when viewing various landscape scenes, although he was not able to account for this difference by changing conditions of illumination. In his laboratory, he showed male graduate students the fold-out page of *Playboy* Magazine. Dramattic dilation was observed. Female pupils dilated to pictures of nude males. The nude dilation effect was reversed for those who reported being homosexual. Yet to be explained was the finding that males tend to contract at the sight of pregnant women. Members of both sexes contracted to photographs of injured children and concentration camp scenes. Conclusions from these studies are: positive emotional experience creates pupil dilation; negative emotional experience induces pupil constriction. In questioning a witness, in interviewing a client and in taking a deposition, the scrutiny of pupil dilation and constriction can be a useful technique to discover whether the attorney's question is having an impact in a negative or positive direction.

A potentially useful measure of emotional change to questioning is the voice print which yields a spectogram, an electronic plotting of vocal sounds with a series of lines.* During the Arab-Israeli war of 1967, voice print was used by the Israeli Government to prove they had intercepted a radio communication of President Nassar of Egypt asking King Hussein of Jordan to support a fictitious allegation that U.S. planes were assisting the Israelis. The voice print proved the radio voices in fact belonged to the Arab

---

*The Spectograph Recorder is sold by Voice Prints Laboratories, P. O. Box 835, Somerville, N. J. 08876.

leaders. Voice print has been successfully used by police detectives to identify criminals who make airline bomb threats, kidnap ransom demands and extortion threats. A psychological stress evaluator (PSE) * has been developed which monitors changes in voice print patterns indicating stressful responses by criminal defendants from which inferences can be drawn regarding deception.

The length of time which passes between the time the attorney asks a witness questions and the time at which the witness responds can be measured by a stop watch. This has significance for discovering fact situations, instances of lying or perceptual distortions. This principle is based on studies in perceptual defense. Psychologist McGinnies found that socially disapproved words such as "whore," "bitch" and "raped" required a greater time for recognition when presented to an individual than more socially neutral words. That is not to say the individual doesn't hear the words spoken, only that he tends to repress them unconsciously. Delay in response, or where the witness asks the attorney to repeat the question suggests a content area of conflict for the witness, and he or she should be examined further about the subject matter of the question. Psychologists have used this technique of measuring time to respond to critical words in a free association test.

Facial expressions are cues to emotional and motivational states, although they are not always correctly deciphered. This point is demonstrated by an Iowa case where a young man was accused of raping a mentally retarded child. The only witnesses for the state were the parents of the child. Their incriminating testimony was based on conversations with the child. The defendant was not a witness in his own behalf. In his closing argument to the jury, the prosecuting attorney said, "While the tale of shame and disgrace unfolds, the defendant sits there smiling and grinning at the child, apparently gloating over his conquest." Defense counsel objected on the basis that the comments were improper since they referred to material that couldn't be placed in the record. The trial court overruled the objection. This holding was sustained by the appellate court which opined that the jury could compare the prosecutors observations with their own.

---

*PSE is sold by Dektor, 5508 Port Royal Road, Springfield, Virginia 22151.
State vs. McKinnon, 138 N.W. 523.

While most people believe they can correctly identify emotional expressions without reference to the context in which they are elicited, behavioral research indicates that they cannot. Can you distinguish facial expressions of surprise from terror, hostility from mirth? Although reactions to emotionally provoking evidence cannot be interpreted validly, many attorneys attempt to enter such material into evidence. In a California case[56] the defendant was charged with a brutal murder. The corpse was not recovered for a protracted period. To demonstrate the horror of the crime, the State offered into evidence a blood-stained seat cover and a human tooth. Testimony was admitted that the defendant's car smelled of putrefying blood. Photographs of the victim's body were shown to the jury which revealed decomposition and tissue areas eaten away by maggots. Three severed fingers of the victim were also introduced. The appellate court ruled that the trial judge should have excluded such evidence to avoid possible prejudice.

Authentic photographs of objects, persons or events are admissible when properly sponsored and bolstered by sufficient predicate. Juries should be warned that photographs can never be isomorphic reproductions or duplications of events. The camera represents only one perspective which is often misleading, just as a single sentence from a deposition can distort meaning. Colored photos may also lack realism because the chemical process of development creates deeper, richer, more saturated hues and varies brightness while blurring the surrounding context.

The effect of context on perception was demonstrated by Professor Sherif by use of the autokinetic illusion. Individuals were brought into a completely darkened room except for the projection of a small beam of light from a black box. The beam of light creates an illusion since without stable frames of reference such as objects in a room, table, chairs, etc., the beam of light appears to wander. Not surprisingly, by telling individuals what direction to expect the light to move toward and at what rate, they report seeing it move according to their expectations, cues and suggestions. In reality, the light does not move at all. The two circles within

---

56. 282 P. 2d 53

the constellations of circles shown here also emphasize contextual effects. The two enclosed circles have identical diameters.

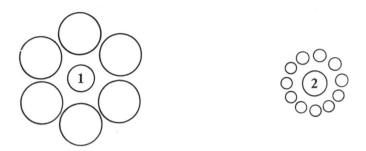

Physical surroundings can affect the nature of perception and judgments when viewing explicitly sexual material. Having viewed such material for the purposes of testifying in several pornography cases including the trial of the movie *Deep Throat*, I have concluded that observing such a movie in a downtown theater on a Saturday night may yield a radically different reaction than when viewing the same movie in court. In court, the sight of the judge in black robes, police uniforms and members of the press, creates guilt feelings for the jurors who may feel ostracism of their neighbors or the criticism of their church if they vote that such a movie has redeeming social value. Prosecutors often capitalize on this fear by giving members of the press the names of jurors in the hope that they may be published in the morning news.

Unconscious motivational factors induce spurious or distorted testimony which the witness consciously believes to be accurate. Untrue confessions induced through guilt, anxiety or masochism, become cathartic for the confessor who is unconsciously confessing to others deeds which he believes require accountability. In American culture, punishment somehow assuages guilt. There was the famous Boorne Case in Vermont, where two brothers confessed to having killed their brother-in-law and also supplied considerable detail as to how the body was disposed of. Years later the "corpus delecti" returned to the scene of the alleged crime. Their psychological guilt over not being able to save their father from a lake drowning was displaced by an admission to another crime.

On the other hand, legal guilt may not represent psychological guilt for mentally ill persons. I once examined a young man who had killed a friend by repeatedly stabbing him. The psychotic defendant's delusional system persuaded him that the friend was possessed by the devil and that a new world of peace could only be realized through exorcism. During the examination, he insisted he was a hero and a savior. He minimized his legal culpability and extolled his action as righteous. When I interviewed his mother, I discovered that her psychological guilt over her son's violent and brutal act was too much for her to bear. She had regressed into a psychosis to deal with it. She explained to me that she visited her son at the County Jail, but that the youth brought to her was not her son—it was the devil physically manifest as her son to deceive her.

Psychoanalyst Theodore Reik explained that the compulsion to make untrue confessions reveals the suspect's attempt to regain a lost love object. It represents an unconscious wooing for love and desire for re-entering society by declaring one is deserving of punishment. The result can be tragic. While consulting at the Texas facility for the criminally insane, I met a prisoner who had confessed to the murder of a minister. He was indicted by a grand jury. Subsequently, he was found insane at the time of trial and was committed to that facility until his mental health was restored. He would then stand trial for the charge of murder. Some months after commitment, another man confessed to the same crime, and police later established that he had actually committed the crime. Since the prisoner was deeply disturbed, his doctors informed me it was unlikely that he would be certified mentally competent in the near future so that he could be returned to court and exonerated.

To be admissible in evidence, confessions must be in writing and signed by the confessor except when they fall within a legal exception. *"Res gestae"* is such an exception. *Res gestae,* which means "excited utterance," is admissible when a judge finds the the statement was made spontaneously while the declarant was under the stress of an exciting event. Professor Wigmore described the rule's justification: "In the stress of nervous excitement, the reflective faculties may be stilled and the utterance may become the unreflecting and sincere expression of one's actual impressions and belief." An example would be, "My God, I must have been speeding," or "I just killed a man." Contrary to Professor Wigmore's explanation, a statement made under stress, resulting from and immediately following a traumatic incident, is more likely to involve inaccuracy and distortion, although the individual may be motivated to tell the truth. A related exception to the inadmissibility of heresay evidence is the "dying declaration." The dying declaration such as "Wilson shot me" is supposedly trustworthy because of the victim's fear of death. The Uniform Rules of Evidence states that the dying declaration is admissible when the speaker is dead and a judge finds his statement was made "voluntarily and in good faith and while the declarant was conscious of his impending death and believed that there was no hope for recovery." Psychologist Edwin S. Shneidman observes that death is "the termination of one's love affair with his own consciousness," and that "brain death as measured by heart beat and the exchange of gases between the person and his environment is always followed by psychological cessation." He challenges the idea that an individual knows he is about to die. Taken a step further, even if an individual could anticipate his own death as in suicide, would that necessarily tend to make his perceptions more accurate or his motives more altruistic? Physicist Percy Bridgman has remarked that the private experiences of death must be distinguished: one can privately experience the public death of a friend; the individual and his friend can privately experience someone else's death; but neither can experience his own death. Death then becomes a phenomenon which can only happen to someone else. Dr. Shneidman notes:[57]

> If you can never experience your own death, it follows logically that you can never experience your own dying. "Now wait a minute," you might say, "granted that I cannot experience my being dead, but obviously I am still alive while I am dying, and unless I am unconscious, I can experience that." The fact is that you can never be certain that you are dying. "Dying" takes its only legitimate meaning from the fact that it immediately precedes death. You may think that you are dying, and then survive, in which case you were not

57. Reprinted from PSYCHOLOGY TODAY Magazine, August, 1970, Copyright © 1970 by Communications/Research/Machines, Inc.

dying at that time. You can, of course, at the present moment keenly experience your belief that you are dying, and the experience can be deathly real. You can also, in the present, anticipate what will happen after you are dead. But these anticipations are at the time they occur always present-moment, live experiences.

Invalid as *res gestae* and dying declarations may be as exceptions to the hearsay rule, admissions of guilt or fault by silence or silence accompanied by a gesture are even more tenuous. The fallacy of admissions by gesture is revealed in the following excerpt from a New York case:[58]

*Question:* Doctor, did you have a conversation with Ernest in the presence of Norma Bill at the Niedert farmhouse just before you left on the night of January 12?
*Answer:* Yes.
*Question:* What did that conversation consist of in your part and on his?
*Answer:* I said to Mr. Bill, "Is there any doubt in your mind that your son committed suicide?" And if I might describe the situation, he and his wife were sitting at the table, mourning and tearful, and he just shook his head.
*Question:* In what direction, Doctor, if you will say it so that the record can pick it up?
*Answer:* A lateral motion of the head.
*Question:* That is commonly interpreted as a negative sign?
*Answer:* Which I interpreted as a negative sign.

*Court:* That the Plaintiff, Ernest Bill, had no doubt that his son had committed suicide was an admission against interest.

The nature of proof in criminal and civil cases is by the process of inference, although Anglo-Saxon jurisprudence recognized "facts" or "statements" of certainty. In science, all evidence is considered circumstantial, as tending to support or negate in probability terms, a phenomenon's occurrence, or a cause and effect relationship.

---

58. 119 N. W. 2d 768.

Proving the criminal defendant guilty by circumstantial proof is fraught with danger. Once while consulting on a criminal case for the defense, I listened to a district attorney explain to the jury how he would prove the defendant murdered the deceased circumstantially. By illustration, he observed that the wooden-topped table at which he stood didn't just appear from out of the blue. From the wooden table top, he would infer a tree, a carpenter, a saw, a sander, etc. The jury seemed to understand his point. During recess I reminded defense counsel that the top of the table was not wooden at all, but was made of a formica sheet which beautifully resembled rich wood grain. Defense counsel used the prosecutor's example in closing argument to illustrate the fallacy and danger of circumstantial proof. The defendant was acquitted.

## EXPERT TESTIMONY

Psychologists are reticent to accept referrals to evaluate and treat a patient embroiled in a law suit or who is accused of a crime. Most have experienced or known colleagues who have been embarrassed or frustrated on the witness stand because they were not able to describe their findings and recommendations in a straightforward, helpful way. Responsibility for this predicament is placed on opposing counsel who the psychologist perceives as attempting to distort, confound or discredit his work. He consequently is skeptical of the adversary process and especially the cross examination as a less than ideal medium for revealing the truth. The reluctance of psychologists to get involved in the legal process robs the jury and the court of the opportunity to hear expert evaluation and prognosis which can help them reach useful, meaningful and just decisions. The attorney who relies on the psychologist's opinion must persuade him not to take the cross examination personally. The psychologist must understand that opposing counsel has essentially only three purposes: to discredit the doctor's credentials, his findings, and the doctor as a person. Attorneys must take the time to meet with the psychologist prior to testimony and explain what is expected of him, what kinds of questions he is likely to be asked and what special challenges and procedural issues he is likely to be confronted with.

When the attorney wishes to present expert psychological testimony to the jury or to the court, the following problems should be discussed with the psychologist so that he may be prepared for the unexpected during pretrial preparation or during cross examination.

1. *Disclosure of findings prior to court appearance.*
   A psychologist will never purposefully violate a patient's confidentiality by disclosing his findings without the patient's permission. Nevertheless, mistakes in judgment occur because of misinformation. For example, the doctor receives a call: "This is Mr. Jones at the District Attorney's office. I would like to know whether you found X to be insane. I certainly wouldn't ask you to do anything improper." In a civil case, a lawyer might call and say, "Doctor, you might as well tell me over the phone what you found. Otherwise, I have to take your deposition and subpoena you anyway."

2. *What's the difference between a psychologist and a psychiatrist?*
   In jurisdictions where psychologists infrequently appear in court, the question may be raised on direct examination. The psychologist should explain the training of the psychiatrist: undergraduate training in natural science, medical school leading to the M.D. degree, internship and residency training in psychiatry. He should then describe the training of the psychologist: undergraduate major in psychology, graduate training leading to the M.S. and Ph.D. degrees in psychology, internship and any other additional training required by his state licensing board. He may explain that the psychiatrist may prescribe medication. The psychologist typically works in association with a physician. In that way, the psychologist's patient may also receive medical care when indicated. The essential opinion question proposed to the psychologist should be: "Doctor, based on your evaluation, have you reached a conclusion as to the 'psychological' state of the defendant?"

3. *What are psychological tests?*
Psychologists often administer psychological tests to aid in diagnosis. The jury must understand that psychological measurements are not "tests" as the word is colloquially used. They are merely information gathering devices to aid in diagnosis. If tests become a subject of testimony, the attorney may wish to bring out that the tests administered are those typically used in hospitals, outpatient clinics and private practices throughout the country. The psychologist should never be placed in the predicament of explaining a single patient response to a single Rorschach card.

4. *"Doctor, aren't you being paid for your testimony?"*
The jury needs to understand that the psychologist is paid for his services in evaluating and treating his patient. These charges should be reasonable with reference to his professional community. The psychologist is paid for his time away from the office, not for his testimony. The judge, the jury and both attorneys are also paid for their time spent in seeking justice.

5. *Are you a treating or a consulting psychologist?*
The attorney who refers a patient to a psychologist should always do so for treatment if indicated after the evaluation. A consultative relationship only is less helpful to the patient and may destroy the concept of privileged communication.

## THE PSYCHOLOGICAL REPORT

As observed in Chapter I, most criminal cases are plea bargained and most civil litigations are settled. For that reason, psychological evidence usually enters the legal process in the form of a report. When requesting a report, the attorney should be certain that the psychologist has secured a release from the client to permit the forwarding of information to him. The attorney should explain to the psychologist the issues which his report should respond to. For example, "Is the patient capable of being an effective parent if custody of the children is given to him?" or "Does emotional disability exist? If so, was it caused by the industrial injury?" The psychologist should make an effort to utilize non-technical language to increase the understanding of attorneys and judges who may need to apply his findings in a practical problem solving way.

Swedish forensic psychologist Arne Trankell in his book, *The Reliability of Evidence,*[59] observes that the meaning and reliability of the psychologist's findings will not have an impact unless he is able to make the significance of his results obvious. Professor Trankell explains that the psychologist's persuasiveness does not only depend on the documentation of findings, but on the ability to express thoughts unequivocably and understandably.

Attorney James Marshall in his book, *Psychology and Law In Conflict,*[60] observes that except in commercial cases, the greatest measure of all evidence introduced in court is eyewitness testimony. The assumption underlying such evidence, he notes, is fallacious—that witnesses can see, hear and recall accurately. The effective attorney recognizes that what is compelling evidence for him is inconclusive for another, and contradictory for still another. He recognizes the limitations for the sense modalities, and the fact that as the stimulus situation becomes more ambiguous, the role of psychological factors such as attitudes, personality, past experience, set motives and emotions becomes more dominant. Most civil cases are ambiguous or they would not be litigated. There are latitudes of uncertainty even in so called "open and shut" criminal cases. The purpose of this chapter has been to introduce the attorney to the principles which effect the persuasiveness of oral and demonstrative evidence.

---

59. A. Trankell, RELIABILITY OF EVIDENCE, Stockholm Rotobeckman A. B., 1972, pp. 159-60.
60. J. Marshall, PSYCHOLOGY AND LAW IN CONFLICT, Bobbs—Merrill Co., New York, 1966, p. 8.

# index

Dr. Robert Gordon grew up in Highland Park, Illinois, the son of an attorney. He earned his bachelor's degree from the University of Wisconsin and his master's and doctorate degrees in psychology at the University of Oklahoma. Fascinated by Munsterberg's turn-of-the-century studies on the psychology of testimony, he was challenged to contribute to the development of the new science of forensic psychology, which strives to improve the administration of justice. He attended the Baylor University School of Law, where he earned a juris doctorate degree and became a member of the Texas Bar. His clinical internship was completed at the Veteran's Hospital at Waco, Texas.

Dr. Gordon founded the *Journal of Forensic Psychology,* and currently practices forensic and clinical psychology in Dallas, Texas, where he has developed a mental health and forensic science clinic. He holds a faculty appointment at Southern Methodist University School of Law, and is Staff Psychologist at Physicians and Surgeons Hospital in Irving, Texas. On a regular basis, he has presented current psychological and legal issues on KERA, educational television. In 1974 Texas Governor Dolph Briscoe appointed him to the State Board of Examiners of Psychologists. He currently serves as president of the International Academy of Forensic Psychology.

Dr. Gordon resides in Dallas with his wife, Susan, and their daughter, Amy.